RECOVERING THE LOST TOOLS
OF LEARNING

TURNING POINT Christian Worldview Series
Marvin Olasky, General Editor

RECOVERING THE LOST TOOLS OF LEARNING

*An Approach to Distinctively
Christian Education*

Douglas Wilson

CROSSWAY BOOKS • WHEATON, ILLINOIS
A DIVISION OF GOOD NEWS PUBLISHERS

Recovering the Lost Tools of Learning:
An Approach to Distinctively Christian Education

Copyright © 1991 by Douglas Wilson.

Published by Crossway Books, a division of
Good News Publishers, Wheaton, Illinois 60187.

 Published in association with the
Fieldstead Institute
P.O. Box 19061,
Irvine, California 92713

Cover Illustration: Guy Wolek

First printing, 1991

Printed in the United States of America

Unless otherwise noted, Bible quotations are taken from *Holy Bible: New
International Version*, copyright © 1978 by the New York International Bible
Society. Used by permission of Zondervan Bible Publishers.

Scripture references designated (NKJV) are taken from the *New King James
Version*. Copyright © 1982, Thomas Nelson, Inc., Publishers. Used by
permission.

Library of Congress Cataloging-in-Publication Data
Wilson, Douglas, 1951-
　　Recovering the Lost Tools of Learning: An Approach to Distinctively
Christian Education
　Douglas Wilson
　　　p. cm. — (Turning point Christian worldview series)
Includes bibliographical references and index
　　1. Moral Education—United States. 2. Education—United
Sates—Aims and objectives. 3. Christian ethics—Study and
teaching—United States. 4. School improvement programs—United
States. I. Title. II. Series.
LC311.W55 1991　　　370'.11'04—dc20　　　　　90-29904
ISBN 0-89107-583-6

99	98	97	96	95	94	93	92	91
15	14	13	12	11	10	9	8	7	6	5	4	3	2	1

Dedicated to
Nancy

I rise up and "call her blessed."

Proverbs 31:28

TABLE OF

CONTENTS

ACKNOWLEDGMENTS

Without the incredible sacrifices made over the last ten years by all the staff and board of Logos School, this book would not have been worth writing. Particular thanks go to Tom Garfield for his dedicated leadership in all the work of Logos School.

I gratefully acknowledge the contribution made by my secretary, Chris LaMoreaux. In addition, those who read over the chapters in their various stages of readiness have my deep gratitude: Terry Morin, Fred Banks, and my wife, Nancy Wilson. Tradition requires that at this point I assert that any mistakes that remain are my own, and, being a traditionalist, it is a service I gladly perform. I would also like to thank my editor, Marvin Olasky, for his insights and his great patience.

My three children, Bekah, Nathan, and Rachel, have been a joyful encouragement to all the work I have done in the field of education. It is not a subject I would have taken up had God not given me the pleasure and responsibility of being their father.

PART ONE

THE FAILURE OF MODERN SECULAR EDUCATION

O N E

THE EDUCATION CRISIS

A young man is sitting at a table, staring at the job application in front of him. He is chewing nervously on the pencil, laboriously struggling through the instructions. He gets up slowly, taking the form with him. Someone at home will have to help him with it. He is a high school graduate.

Susan is delivering her small child to a birthday party in a part of town unfamiliar to her. She has to take a friend along with her because she can't read the street signs. She dropped out of high school in the tenth grade. If ten years is not good enough, then what difference will two more make?

A business executive throws down a pile of papers in frustration. He has just received a report that his company will have to invest in a costly program of remedial instruction for its employees. A high school diploma is no longer a guarantee that an individual is ready to start work. He stares at the ceiling, wondering what has happened to the public school system.

My oldest daughter Bekah is now in the ninth grade. While she was still a toddler, my wife and I realized that sending her to the public schools was not an option for us. My wife commented that she just could not hand our daughter over to someone we didn't know and say, "Here she is, educate her." I agreed wholeheartedly. At that time our community had no adequate alternative to the public school system. I told Nancy that we would have a Christian school by the time Bekah started kindergarten. It is hard to imagine anyone knowing less about education than I did at the time, but God is kind to the ignorant—provided they acknowledge it and are willing to learn.

I joined two other like-minded parents, and we began meeting regularly to pray, investigate, and plan.[1] As I look back, it is amazing to me that Logos School opened in my daughter's kindergarten year with nineteen students. Today we have over two hundred students, with many exciting prospects for the future. We have learned many lessons. One of the first surprises was discovering that we were part of a national movement toward private education. But at the time we were not trying to join any movement; we were simply trying to be good parents.[2]

That is the key to understanding this book. This is a book about education, but it is not written by a professional educator. I have not one education degree to my name and no current plans to acquire one. Nor is this book written for professional educators, although I believe many of them could profit by it. I am writing this book as a parent—*an involved parent*.[3] I am writing to parents who would like to be involved in the education of their children and to parents who already are involved, but who want to be more effective. What does it take? It takes a lot more than you think and a lot less than you think.

HARD WURDS

When I first got involved in education around 1978, many of my concerns about the public school system were intuitive; I had a general, unresearched awareness that there were serious academic problems. But as the eighties progressed, study after study continued to reveal the extent of the problems, some of which were the result of previously implemented reforms.[4] Today few would dispute that public education in America has run into hard times, although there is debate over the reasons for it. Surveys concerning our students' lack of basic factual knowledge indicate part of the problem.

The National Commission on Excellence in Education (NCEE) reported that the schooling of the average student is barely adequate and that one out of every seven seventeen-year-olds in the United States is functionally illiterate.[5] Reading ability has not been the only casualty. According to a report by the National Academy of Sciences, three out of four students leave school without mastering enough mathematics for ". . . on-the-job demands for problem solving or college expectations for mathematical literacy."[6] Not only do problems exist in math classes generally, they extend into advanced mathematics for seniors. When compared with their classmates, such advanced students would of course do well. But when compared internationally, the picture for such students is even more dismal than for the average student.[7]

In a comparison of 24,000 thirteen-year-olds from the United States, Ireland, Spain, South Korea, the United Kingdom, and four Canadian provinces, the United States placed last in mathematics and almost last in science. Korean students were first in math and tied for first in science with Canadian students[8] in British Columbia.[9] In one aspect of math, however, the Americans did just fine. "Despite their poor overall performance, however, two-thirds of U. S. thirteen-year-olds felt that 'they are good at mathematics'; only 23 percent of their Korean counterparts shared that attitude."[10] When it comes to maintaining a high self-image, we can take on the world.[11]

In science, there seems to be a general consensus that reform efforts do not have much time.[12] Between now and the year 2000, our system of higher education will produce 450,000 too few Bachelors of Science.[13] Obviously this shortage of science majors in college is a problem that begins much earlier. One national survey of 1,200 U. S. schools found that they teach science in the primary grades for only eighteen minutes a day.[14]

History and geography fare no better. More than half of American students graduate from high school without having studied Western civilization or world history.[15] *National Geographic* has launched a national "geography bee" to help combat the swelling tide of geographic ignorance.[16] A number of years ago, Sam Cook had a humorous pop love song called "Wonderful World." One of the lines was ". . . don't know much about history." Little did he know his song was going to become our national anthem.[17] Of course, this shouldn't be surprising. History is learned from books, and with declining reading skills, the textbooks have been "dumbed down."[18] As reading skills vanish, the ability to write coherently is also disappearing.

Dropping out is another problem—or rather a symptom of the same problem. If attending school will not result in literacy, then why not drop out? In 1988, of the 3.8 million Americans who were eighteen, fully 700,000 had dropped out of school. Another 700,000 could not read their high school diplomas.[19] Does it really make that much difference whether a child is a dropout or a graduate who can't read?

HELP FROM THE ESTABLISHMENT?

President Bush has let it be known that he wants to be an "education president." One of the steps he has taken toward this goal was calling the nation's governors together for an "education summit," held in Charlottesville, Virginia, in September of 1989. Whatever criticisms can be made of the summit,[20] at least it shows how serious the problem is.[21] A president has not called the nation's governors together in this way since Franklin Roosevelt did so during the Depression. One of the good suggestions offered at this education summit was to compare American students on an international scale. This would prevent the charge that critics of the public school system are looking back to some mythological golden past of the public schools.[22] But as the studies above make clear, if American students *are* compared to their peers overseas, the results are frightening. For another example, only 3.5 percent of American high school seniors could pass the graduation exam of a European academic high school.[23]

Some educators recognize the problem, but deny that it is a new one. "The problem of basic incompetence in high school reading and writing is emphatically not a new problem; neither is it a budding educational or social catastrophe. It is only more shameful and embarrassing now that it has been brought to light again by new studies; and because we spend so much money on the schools, we think we have the right to expect fewer failures from them."[24] And yet, in spite of their comment, these same authors are forced to recognize that a real decline in education is not just an illusion resulting from more research.[25] Protests now arise from all segments of the political spectrum. For example, Peter McLaren, an assistant professor of education at Miami University in Ohio, has joined the chorus lamenting the "rampant illiteracy," but he lists it in a larger catalog of ills ranging from resurgent racism and elitism to a disintegrating ozone layer.[26] In other words, the schools are getting so bad that some of the trendiest on the left can see it.

WHAT, ME WORRY?

Some educators think we are doing a good job teaching basic skills and are wondering what all the fuss is about.[27] "Although the goal of universal literacy has not yet been achieved, great progress has been made. Taking the long view, it is clear that the American educational system has been amazingly responsive to societal expectations. Furthermore, the schools particularly have been responding to the ever-increasing demand for literacy."[28] Consider this profound observation by the same writer, "In reviewing the expectations that society holds for the educational system, it is evident that the area of literacy has been considered the special responsibility of the school."[29] If we think how this type of logic would sound if applied to other jobs or professions, it is less surprising that we have an educational crisis on our hands; i.e., ". . . in reviewing the expectations that society holds for fire departments, it is evident that the area of putting out fires has been considered the special responsibility of the fire departments." The fact that society expects schools to teach reading is considered a profound insight. What we have here is a failure to communicate.[30] In some quarters of the education world, there is a growing truculence[31] combined with befuddlement. "Blaming the schools has become a national pastime. . . . And when reading skills are found to be deficient among large numbers of people, once again the schools are blamed."[32] Yes, many students can't read, but why is everyone blaming the schools?

The crisis has even made the big screen. Two movies have been made recently about our collapsing educational system and the endeavors of two individuals to do something about it. *Lean On Me* is about Joe Clark, a much praised and much vilified (former) high school principal in Paterson, New Jersey. The story records how through strict discipline Clark cleaned up a slum of a school and made quite a few enemies. Hint: the enemies were not limited to the drug dealers he kicked off campus; they included a few in the education establishment.[33] In *Stand and Deliver*, Hollywood has given us an academic *Rocky*. An inspiring teacher in East L.A. refuses to give up on his math students and takes them all the way to the Calculus Advanced Placement exam. Films like this testify to the fact that the crisis in education has entered the popular consciousness. *Dirty Harry* meant there was a popular awareness of a crime problem; movies like these indicate the same about education.

A LITTLE SLEEP, A LITTLE SLUMBER . . .

The danger is great, for as the NCEE report made clear, history is not kind to idlers, and educationally we are a nation of idlers. As should be expected, the problem in the inner cities is much worse. *Newsweek* magazine reported on the school system in Chicago and described it as "near meltdown."[34] The illiteracy rate among minority youth may run as high as 40 percent.[35] Some inner-city parents are desperate.

For example, in Chicago, some parents save up enough money to rent an apartment in a suburban district long enough to establish residency—one month. Then they move back to the inner city, hoping their children can continue in a decent school. One district there has truant officers monitor suburban-bound commuter trains in order to catch such kids.[36] Obviously, Thomas Sowell had a point when he wrote that educational change is most vital for "those who are mentioned least: the poor, the working class, and all whose children are trapped in educationally deteriorating and physically dangerous public schools."[37]

Of course it is not possible to see the problem of struggling students without at some point questioning the teaching profession. For example, in March of 1986, all public school teachers in Texas were given a test in basic writing and reading. The state teachers' association fought the testing program unsuccessfully in the courts. When that effort failed, a massive effort was launched to prepare the teachers for the test. When the test results came in, education officials were overjoyed and danced like Miriam beside the Red Sea. Only 6,579 teachers (3.3 percent) had failed the basic reading and writing test![38]

It is clear that competent individuals must be attracted to the teaching profession if the public schools are to be salvaged. What is less clear is the fact that competent teachers are currently being driven out. For example, qualified teachers are reacting to the byzantine maze of certification requirements in a very simple way—they leave. Requiring teachers to be competent is one thing, but requiring them to take education courses can be quite another. Do teachers really need to take lessons on how to pass out paper?[39] And how can we expect to attract new people to the teaching profession when typical certification requirements keep someone with an M.A. in English from teaching English?

The situation is pretty dismal. But the picture is even bleaker than one would think, for there may have been widespread cheating in the administration of standardized tests.[40] The cheating results in what is called the Lake Wobegone Effect: all the states have children who are above average. There are apparently just two states where the kids aren't above average (Louisiana and Arizona), and that is only because they recently shifted to a different kind of test.[41] The cheating included teachers who "spent the morning teaching the test and the afternoon giving it." It also included improper help for students taking the test, and tampering with the tests after they had been taken. Apparently, some educators are pretty desperate.

THE BUSINESS OF AMERICA IS ... TEACHING?

The alarm over the state of education is widespread. Myron Lieberman, who is in the vanguard of education reformers, points out that the calls for reform do not proceed from a handful of disgruntled critics. He says, with regard to the National Commission on Excellence in Education, " ... the list of advisers and consultants for this report alone reads like a Who's Who in education."[42] Business leaders are alarmed as well. Faced with a shrinking pool of qualified workers, they question whether American business can compete effectively with foreign business. The problem is exacerbated by the fact that the number of people entering the work force is shrinking in real numbers,[43] and those coming around for jobs have not been adequately trained.

Joan Ratteray, president of the Institute for Independent Education, asks why business is so tolerant of the status quo in public education. What if education *were* a business? She says, "A public high school teacher from Cincinnati, James Arata, dramatized the point this way: He has asked us to compare our school systems with a monopolistic industry that has doubled its work force while its customer base was shrinking, an industry where total expenditures have tripled and unit-production costs have quadrupled over the last three decades. However, one-third of its products are seriously defective, another third noticeably deficient, and the best 5 percent are only average when compared to items produced in Japan."[44]

Jerry Hume, a member of the California Business Roundtable education task force, put the problem this way: "Many school systems today are providing a product that nobody willingly would pay for if they had a choice. ... Businesses acknowledge it by spending billions of dollars each year to teach employees the basic math and reading skills they should have acquired before they entered the world of work."[45]

A BROADER ILLITERACY

In his book *Cultural Literacy*, E. D. Hirsch argues that current woes are not limited to a lack of ability with letters. Even among students who can read, the problem of *cultural* illiteracy exists. Hirsch places the responsibility for this mess on the "fragmented curriculum" of today's public schools. As a result of our deteriorating schools, many students do not have the background of information that every educated American should possess. Hirsch argues that basic literacy is only a beginning and that cultural literacy requires that the student learn large amounts of specific information. Sadly, our schools are not doing a good job with either type of literacy.

Of course when education doesn't educate, it becomes impossible for the students in such a system to enjoy the fruit that education used to produce. One example of such a loss is the declining love of great books. Allan Bloom commented on the problem. "At all events, whatever the cause, our students have lost the practice of and the taste for reading. . . . When I first noticed the decline in reading during the late sixties, I began asking my large introductory classes, and any other group of younger students to which I spoke, what books really count for them. Most are silent, puzzled by the question."[46] Bloom is talking about a problem that becomes manifest in higher education, but it obviously began much earlier in the educational process.

DO WE WANT TOO MUCH?

Have we perhaps set our expectations too high? Is it unrealistic to suppose that everyone can be literate? Can a *nation* be educated? Or even worse, is the drive for universal literacy horribly misguided? Some think that the concern over things like this is nothing more than some sort of middle class imperialism. "Thus the pragmatic dimension of American literacy has been sanctified. It has become a tyrannical object of mysterious veneration."[47]

History answers the question for us, and the answer is that our expectations are *not* too high. Our second president, John Adams, referred to the fact that "a native in America, especially of New England, who cannot read and write is as rare a phenomenon as a comet."[48] A report to the third president, Thomas Jefferson, concluded that "[n]ot more than four in a thousand [young Americans] are unable to write legibly—even neatly. . . . "[49] The report gave credit for this state of affairs in America to the practice of Bible reading, as well as to the reading of newspapers.

In 1850, the illiteracy rate in Europe was 50 percent (60 percent if Russia was included). In the United States at that time the illiteracy rate was only 22 percent, and that was counting the slaves. If the slaves were not counted, the illiteracy rate was less than 11 percent, and for large subgroups like male New Englanders, the rate approached zero.[50]

It is clear that the crisis we are in is not a necessary state of affairs. Children are taller now than they were two hundred years ago; there is no reason to believe they have shrunk mentally. But the problems go even deeper than has been suggested so far. The breakdown of discipline has not been limited to academics. Many schools are no longer even *safe* places to be.[51] A generation or two ago, discipline problems in the schools concerned things like running in the halls or chewing gum. Today, students and teachers alike have to be concerned about assault, rape, and murder. Drug abuse is rampant, and despite the emphasis on sex education, sexual immorality and teenage pregnancy are major problems.

HOW SHOULD WE THEN TEACH?

I said at the beginning that this book was written by an involved parent, for involved parents. But there is one other thing. It is not enough to care for children sincerely; the care must also be informed, and for Christians, it is important to build on the foundation of a Biblical worldview. The more controversial an issue is, the more important it is to have your Biblical bearings. This book will develop, step by step, a Biblical response to educational breakdown. In the next chapter, we will closely examine the various proposals for the reform of the public schools and make some suggestions based on Biblical principles. School prayer will be examined as an archetypical example of this effort.

A second section will address the Biblical presuppositions essential in the development of a distinctively Christian education. We will begin with a chapter on the true department of education— the family. We will go on to discuss the nature of knowledge, the nature of the student, and the limitations of knowledge.

A third section will cover the question of what constitutes a distinctively classical education. We will look at what is meant by the phrase, "the classical mind." We will then discuss the nature of the curriculum and the efforts of Logos School to follow the pattern set down by Dorothy Sayers in her essay, "The Lost Tools of Learning." But because education does not take place in a world governed by the classical ideal, we will also discuss the various obstacles of modernity—obstacles presented by the students and the world. We will then go on to the problem of "pious ignorance," i.e., the belief of some Christians that scholarship and academic excellence should be viewed with suspicion. The options of home schooling and private Christian schools will be discussed, with a look at some of the pitfalls of each.

A fourth section will summarize the arguments and show that a truly Biblical education can be provided by parents anywhere. As we consider the 1990s and the approaching twenty-first century, we must realize that our only link with the future is through our children. There is no way to think Biblically about the education of our children without thinking of future generations.

SUGGESTED SECULAR AND CHRISTIAN REFORMS

QUO VADIS? WHICH WAY?

*T*he nation is at an educational impasse but not because no one has any idea of what to do. On the contrary, suggested reforms are legion. While there is general agreement that we have a problem,[1] the consensus breaks down when we come to specific solutions. As the NCEE commented archly, "The Commission was impressed during the course of its activities by the diversity of opinion it received regarding the condition of American education and by conflicting views about what should be done."[2]

There are three major categories of reformers. Those with a more secular mind-set advocate two types of reforms—structural and curricular. The structural reformers want to adjust pay scales, give schools more autonomy, etc. Curricular reformers believe that we must return to the rigorous academic standards of an earlier era and get "back to the basics." The third category consists of "moral reformers," who push for a return to basic Judeo/Christian moral traditions; they want to get prayer *back* in the classroom and get values clarification and condoms *out*.

It should be immediately obvious that these divisions are not watertight. There is no reason why a structural reformer would not support rigorous academic standards, for example; and it certainly would be unfair to suggest that academic reformers are opponents of morality. I have made these divisions simply as a reflection of the emphases found in the writings of the various reformers. At the same time, the secular reformers do have a tendency to support a return to "traditional values" in the classroom because of their utilitarian value. Discipline is necessary for a rigorous education, and morality is necessary to maintain discipline. Those who are serious about moral reform for its own sake are considered in a separate section.

STRUCTURAL REFORM

One approach to reform suggests that the problem is largely in the way our schools are run. Let's briefly survey four of the leading "structural reform" proposals.[3]

More Money

One of the few structural reforms that has been supported by the education establishment is the call for more money. When mainstream educators admit problems, they usually argue that our public schools are not funded adequately. If the schools had enough money, *then* the job would get done. Even those who insist on more substantive reforms than this will usually list better funding as one of the reforms to be achieved. For example, the NCEE report said, "We also call upon citizens to provide the financial support necessary to accomplish these purposes. Excellence costs. But in the long run mediocrity costs far more."[4] This thought is summed up by the bumper sticker which says, "If you think education is expensive, try ignorance." I have been tempted to print a bumper sticker in response that says, "We did try ignorance, and now it wants a raise."

The nation's largest and most powerful union, the National Education Association (NEA), fully backs this assertion that the problem can largely be understood as a lack of funds. Michael Kirst, a past president of the California Board of Education, writing in an NEA publication, says, "Excellence costs. No other assertion in the entire debate on education reform is more on target, further beyond dispute. And yet many people . . . do dispute this claim. . . . The deplorable condition of many of today's schools—the scarce resources, the underpaid staffs, the sparse curriculums, the unsafe facilities—proves again that excellence costs and that the states cannot adequately meet those costs."[5]

Fortunately, money being the quantifiable thing that it is, this is one suggestion that can easily be checked. Lack of money does not appear to be a factor in the decline of academic achievement. For example, in the school year 1959/60, the total expenditure per pupil in the United States was $1,699, while in 1985/86, the figure had risen to $3,937 (and these amounts are in constant 1985/86 dollars). And what was happening to test scores over a portion of the same period? In 1966/67, the SAT average for college-bound seniors was 958. By 1985/86, the scores had fallen to 906.[6] In other words, test scores are falling, money is being spent furiously, and the lack of results is beginning to look like a permanent fixture.

Nevertheless, groups like the NEA are adamant that more money is needed. Those who suggest this as a serious reform fail to realize that one of the reasons people are so dissatisfied with our schools in the first place is the fact that so much money is spent on them. If an average private school were given the same amount of money per pupil as an average public school gets, they wouldn't know what to do with it all. If excellence costs so much, then how is it possible for so many shoe-string private academies to turn out students that do so well academically?[7]

Better Motivation to Attract Teachers

Considering what has just been said, the next proposal regarding education reform is unlikely to win endorsement from the NEA. Charles Murray, in *In Pursuit of Happiness and Good Government*, argues that one of the culprits in our education disaster is *high* salaries for teachers: ". . . increase in pay will make it only slightly less sacrificial for the talented to be teachers, but much more attractive for the second-rate to become teachers."[8] For those used to hearing the repeated calls for more and more funding for public education, this kind of argument may come as something of a shock. But Murray is ready for the anticipated response. ". . . am I really serious in thinking that we could raise teachers' salaries substantially and still not get better teachers? Of course we can. *We've raised teachers' salaries for years without getting better teachers.*"[9]

These are not the vaporings of some theorist, hopelessly out of touch with the real world. Murray goes on to demonstrate his point with hard data.[10] But he is *not* arguing that teachers should be paid less than they are worth. His basic point is that payment cannot be reduced to money. Murray argues that potential teachers are involved in the pursuit of happiness just like everyone else. As they make the decision to enter teaching, they should not be assumed to be after money only. If money is assumed to be the sole motivation, then it will only attract the second-rate.

His argument is that teachers have traditionally never been paid very much. At the same time, he claims they have been highly respected, and that respect is part of the motivation for being a teacher. Not all paychecks can be cashed at the bank. In the public schools of today, however, we have reversed this traditional order. We pay our teachers well, and they are not highly respected. The results are predictable. Murray's thinking here is a variant of the Biblical principle that hirelings care nothing for the sheep (John 10:7-13).

Now these intangible rewards for teaching cannot be written into a teaching contract. But, Murray would argue, we *can* keep things out of the contracts which clearly interfere with such intangibles: "In other words, I am drawing from this line of reasoning a hypothesis that *the task in solving the teacher problem is not to engineer solutions but to strip away impediments to behaviors that would normally occur*"[11] (the emphasis is Murray's).

Murray regards it as fundamentally *odd* that we have a problem attracting competent teachers for our children. He concludes that our way of doing things must be getting in the way in some strange fashion and that we ought to quit it. Attracting competent people to teach is not some big mystery. It has been done for thousands of years. So why are *we* having trouble with it?

This is not meant to reduce Murray's treatment of education to a mere discussion of salaries. He also is in favor of granting much more parental choice in the selection of schools, which, incidentally, opens the way for parents to get involved in teachers' lives. This is necessary if many of the intangible benefits of teaching are to be given to the teachers. He says: "One of the major virtues of the free-choice system is that it will instantaneously permit those parents to put their children into schools that are run according to their rules."[12]

It is interesting to note that in most private schools, Murray's suggested reform is in place by default; teachers' salaries in private schools are not competitive with those of their public school counterparts. This is not the result of agreement with Murray's thesis necessarily; it is the result of not having very much money. Still, it demonstrates Murray's point. Over the years, I have marveled at how many talented teachers have worked for us at Logos for so little. It has been obvious, again and again, that first-rate teachers are not motivated by money alone.

Reduce Bureaucracy

The third reform proposal deals with the bureaucracy of the education establishment. The Manhattan Institute, a nonpartisan think tank oriented to free-market solutions,[13] has published a small booklet entitled "Making Schools Better." The booklet resulted from a discussion between Nathan Glazer, John Chubb, and Seymour Fliegel about the public schools of New York. It concludes that schools are hindered in their work because of top-heavy bureaucratic administration. For example, John Chubb, a senior fellow at the Brookings Institute tells of his attempt to determine how many people worked in the central office of New York's public schools compared with how many worked in the central office of New York's Catholic school system:

> I called the personnel office of the city school system and said, "I have a simple question: how many people work in the central office of the New York City School System?" The first person I reached had no idea, nor did the second or third, but they all promised to transfer me to someone who did.
>
> Thirty-five minutes and many transfers later, I got to a person who said, "Yes, I do know the number, but if you want to know, you'll have to put your request in writing, send it through the proper channels and we'll get the information back to you in a month."
>
> Well, I pleaded and explained the circumstances, and finally I was put in touch with someone who had the authority and the number. And he told me it wasn't 5,000; it was 6,000.

Chubb then turned his attention to the Catholic school system. He phoned someone in the central office and asked her some questions which were promptly answered. He then said:

> "The last thing I need to know is how many people work in the central bureaucracy of the Catholic school system in New York City."
>
> And she said, "I'm sorry, we don't keep that kind of data."
>
> "Well," I said, "would you have any idea? Is there any way you could get the number for me?"
>
> And she said: "Just a minute—I'll count them." And she counted. There are twenty-five. Twenty-five people running a school system that's a fifth to a quarter of the size of the public school system.[14]

Chubb draws an obvious lesson from this. He recognizes that schools must be accountable, but not to a bureaucracy. He argues that the schools must have a degree of autonomy:

The only way to provide autonomy without losing accountability is to go to a different system of accountability. A top-down system will not work. You must build a system of accountability to parents and students rather than to politicians and administrators.

It works in the private sector. Private schools are held accountable to their constituency through the process of competition and choice. Similarly, the surest way to get autonomy and accountability into the public school system is not through regulation and spending, but through a mechanism of choice.[15]

Chubb goes on to specify what he means by "mechanism of choice." He is talking about vouchers, open enrollments, magnet schools, and so forth. These are reforms which would make the schools accountable to a different constituency—parents and students, instead of bureaucrats. For example, if parents didn't like what was going on at one school, they could choose to spend their vouchers at another. While arguing that this sort of freedom from bureaucratic strangulation must be brought to the public system, he recognizes that this freedom already exists in the private sector. "If you don't find autonomy in public schools except under unusual circumstances, you almost always find it in private schools, including religious schools."[16]

In the published discussion, Seymour Fliegel, a former deputy superintendent in the New York public school system,[17] accepts this argument about bureaucracy, but applies it with a twist: "John says do away with bureaucracy. The alternative is to ignore the bureaucracy."[18]

Fliegel's approach is not to reform the system as a whole (at least not right now), but rather to develop pockets of sanity within the system. This can be done by pretending that the bureaucracy doesn't exist:

As I said in the beginning, I think you can take autonomy. But you have to give up certain things. You can't be too ambitious to move up the administrative ladder, because if you are, then the system has something on you. But that is the only hold the system can have. Otherwise nothing ever happens to anyone in the New York City school system. Nobody ever gets fired. So what is there to be afraid of? You've got to be willing to take a bit of a hard time occasionally, that's all.[19]

In other words, with a healthy measure of respect for common sense and a disrespect for bureaucratic authority, individual districts or schools may be reformed. The difficulty with this is that while a centralized bureaucracy can tolerate a maverick or two, there is no way the system *as a whole* can be efficiently reformed in this way. As these gentlemen recognized, the *natural* place where their wisdom about bureaucracy is respected is in the private sector. In private schools, there is a built-in check against unrestrained bureaucratic growth.

Local Control

A common theme among the structural reformers is the necessity of local control over schools. Those who advocate more parental involvement and control have not necessarily always felt this way. The decline in educational standards has resulted in a change of mind for some. For example, in 1960 in *The Future of Public Education*, Myron Lieberman argued that:

> Local control of education has clearly outlived its usefulness on the American scene. Practically, it must give way to a system of educational controls in which local communities play ceremonial rather than policy-making roles. *Intellectually*, it is already a corpse. At least, I propose to treat it as such in this book.[20]

As the years went by, it became apparent that the public school system was in trouble. Mr. Lieberman was not blind, and he was not afraid to change. In 1986, in *Beyond Public Education*, he emphasized the need for local control, and he wrote that:

> Tuition tax credits and vouchers (hereinafter, "family choice proposals" or "tuition tax credits/vouchers") constitute the most significant proposals to improve the process of education through changes in its governance structure.[21]

This reform can be summed up in one word: choice. If parents are enabled through tuition tax credits, or vouchers, to select the school their children attend, then that will bring about competition between the schools for students. Second-rate schools will have to reform or face going out of business. It is this element of choice that appears to be in the forefront of President Bush's agenda for school reform, although he appears to want the choices limited to public schools.[22] Minnesota has a system of choice in place, and Arkansas, Iowa, Ohio, and Nebraska are moving toward choice.[23] Chester

Finn, professor of education and public policy at Vanderbilt University, notes that choice is a "powerful idea," but he also warns that we might be seeing the beginnings of a backlash among educators against the concept.[24]

Nevertheless, it is an idea that is gaining adherents, even in unexpected places. For example, Polly Williams, a state representative in Wisconsin, pushed a voucher plan through the legislature that would allow low-income Milwaukee students to attend private, nonsectarian schools. This is not that remarkable unless you consider that Williams is a black Democrat, who was twice the chair of Jesse Jackson's campaign in Wisconsin. Nevertheless, she has little patience with the suffocating paternalism of the education establishment that is destroying opportunity for inner-city blacks.[25] She has said, "We have to be saved from our saviors." The education establishment in that state has responded with a lawsuit; they want the law struck down as unconstitutional. Williams responded appropriately enough,"If you all are worried about your jobs, try doing them better."[26]

Giving parents the choice presents some private schools with an interesting dilemma. This is a reform which will certainly result in an improvement in the public school system. However, there will be some who insist that parents should be allowed to choose a good private Christian school under this system. But if Christian schools are included, the question of state accreditation will then become an important one. The chances are good that parents will not be able to use tuition tax credits or vouchers at nonaccredited schools. This will create pressure for those private schools to seek state accreditation in order to qualify for these new funds. Yet quite a few private schools will be extremely reluctant to rush right in.[27] In the minds of many, accreditation does not represent quality-control as much as it represents curriculum-control, teacher-training-control, drinking-fountain-height-control, etc. The reason we have reached this dismal state in education is the state's inability to control the quality of education in its *own* schools. It should not be surprising, therefore, if some private educators should decline to give up *their* liberty to choose in order to be a part of "choice reform." A private school that is accredited by the state is, *in principle*, a controlled school.[28]

Nevertheless, those who are concerned for education in America should be heartened, broadly speaking, by the move toward parental choice and local control over education. At the same time, it is not an unmixed blessing. There are potential dangers—this is one reform that is necessary, but it might result in a system needing a different type of reform later.

CURRICULUM REFORM

Those advocating curriculum reform believe our *academic* standards have slipped and slipped badly. The problem is seen in grade inflation, abandonment of a core curriculum, too many electives, falling standards for teachers, etc. If we tightened our standards, the argument goes, we could turn the falling test scores around, restore academic discipline to our schools, and so forth.

The falling standards are attacked in two ways. The first is with a relentless assault of facts: test scores, tables of expenditures, test scores, anecdotes about ignorance, and more test scores. The second way the point is made is through ridicule. This is the approach of countless editorial cartoons. (*"Teechers on stryke!"*) Perhaps the thinking is that the public schools can be embarrassed into change.

Let's briefly survey four approaches to curriculum reform.

Phonics

The most important curriculum reform deals with all learning that involves the written word. This crucial reform concerns the teaching of reading in the first grade. Few outside the world of education have any idea how far away from common sense our teaching of reading has fallen. English is a phonetic language, which a child can quickly learn to read if he or she is taught the sounds of the various letters or combinations of letters. This simple truth represents to some educators a deep mystery. For example, David Harman, an author of two books on the problem of illiteracy, writes:

> There are twenty-six letters in the English alphabet. Just how difficult can it be to learn them, to memorize the sounds that each symbolizes, and to put them together to form words and sentences? . . . Why, then, has the acquisition of reading skills, seemingly so simple, been so evasive? There is, unfortunately, *no easy answer.*[29]

Those who would reform the teaching of reading in American schools would reply, and sometimes with anger, that there *is* an easy answer. The answer is abandonment of the long-discredited "look-say" method of reading instruction and a return to basic instruction in phonics.

In 1955, Rudolf Flesch published *Why Johnny Can't Read*, which explained precisely the problem with reading instruction in U. S. schools. He said, "So, ever since 1500 B. C. people all over the world—wherever an alphabetic system of writing was used—learned how to read and write by the simple process of memorizing the sound of each letter in the alphabet. . . . This is not miraculous, it's the only natural system of learning how to read."[30] Flesch notes that every single nation throughout history with an alphabet taught reading in this way—except "twentieth-century Americans—and other nations insofar as they followed our example. And what do we use instead? . . . We have decided to forget that we write with letters and learn to read English as if it were Chinese."[31]

The educational establishment did not respond well to Flesch's observations. For example, in the NEA *Journal* Flesch was accused of trying to "discredit American education." In November of 1955, the *Journal* published another attack on Flesch entitled "Why Can't Rudy Read."[32] It was apparent rather quickly that Flesch had hit a nerve. Although the NEA *reacted* to his criticism, the continued problems we have with illiteracy show that they did not learn from it. In 1981, Flesch published another book entitled *Why Johnny Still Can't Read*. He reported on the progress since his first book. There hasn't been much. "Unfortunately my advice fell on deaf ears. With heart-breaking slowness, phonics-first crept into some 15 percent of our schools, but an estimated 85 percent of them still stick to old, discredited look-and-say. The results of this mass miseducation have been disastrous. America is rapidly sinking into a morass of ignorance."[33]

In other words, if your first grade child is in the public schools, his potential reading skills are in severe danger. There is an 85 percent chance that he is being taught by a method abandoned 3,500 years ago when the alphabet was invented. It sounds incredible—critics like Flesch face a problem in getting average people to believe that our schools are really doing something so stupid.[34] The look-say method seems so ludicrous, and the phonics method makes so much sense, it seems impossible to believe that our educators reject phonics instruction. But they do. In 1983-4, the NEA stated in *Today's Education* that an overemphasis on phonics for beginners was ready for the "scrap heap."[35] At Logos School, we teach phonics, and we have fewer illiterates coming out of first grade (none, actually) than the public schools have coming out of twelfth grade. Do we really want to throw on the scrap heap a teaching method that works?

Ridicule

It is sometimes difficult to take the education establishment seriously. Richard Mitchell, the "Underground Grammarian," is a practitioner of the reform-through-ridicule approach and an acerbic critic of public education in practice. Nevertheless, he staunchly defends what he believes public schools could be. He does not suffer fools gladly, and his apparent strategy is to reform the system through scorn, the way one would lance a boil. A sample follows. "It is another of the educationists' self-serving delusions that if enough of the ignorant pool their resources, knowledge will appear, and that a parliament of fools can deliberate its way to wisdom."[36]

He does not deliver his suggestions for reform in a quiet, somber, pedantic way. He attacks the stupidity that governs much of our educational system with what seems to be an odd mixture of glee and grief. He comments on the NCEE report on our declining education system. "In the manner of the typical social studies text, which is likely to explain the Civil War by saying that 'problems arose,' the commission's report laments all sorts of bad things that are said to have 'happened' in the schools. The commissioners are perturbed to notice that courses in physics and courses in bachelor living carry the same credit, but hardly the same enrollment, in most schools. That, as they must know, didn't just happen. Persons *did* it, and they did it by design and out of policy."[37]

Mitchell does not believe that reform will come easily or from within the system. "If we *do* want to 'do something' about the schools, we must begin by giving up forever the futile hope that the educationists will do it for us if only we ask them often enough."[38] He is not optimistic. "What can we hope for now that such people have boldly announced their intention to devise new programs of emphasis on the great role of the humanities in the development of Western Civilization and powers of knowledge and critical thought as the necessary virtues of a free society? Nothing. Or, more precisely, nothing but more of the same."[39]

Mitchell does not seem to believe reform is coming any time soon. But in the meantime, he is intent on his task, which is to point out that the superintendent has no clothes and that a motorized attendance module is really a bus.

Return to Basics

The question of curriculum reform cannot be separated from the question of what constitutes true education. We cannot measure progress until we have agreed on our destination. Richard Powers, the author of *The Dilemma of Education in a Democracy*, argues that one of our problems is that academic goals have shifted.

> In the older education the teacher was measured by what he or she could do with a bright girl or boy. . . . For the first time in the history of education teaching came to be measured, not by what could be done with the best, but by what could be done with the worst.[40]

This shift in focus obviously affects the curriculum. What Powers calls the "crusade against intellectualism" succeeded quite well, if you want to call it success. "Latin, taken by 49 percent of all high school students in 1911, was taken by 7.8 percent in 1949. Modern language enrollment fell from 84 percent to 22 percent."[41] The problem was not limited to the study of language. "Algebra enrollment fell from 57 percent to 27 percent. . . . Total mathematics fell from 90 percent to 55 percent, total science enrollment from 82 percent to 33 percent."[42]

Powers gives a cogent argument for reform of our schools' curricula, which must begin with a proper understanding of our academic goals. What *is* education? He traces the decline of educational standards in our country, attacks the egalitarianism foundational to the decline, notes how such egalitarianism destroys true freedom, and then proposes his reforms. But they are not the reforms of a revolutionary. This is someone who wants to turn back to a lost era, arguing that there is no reason it cannot be rediscovered. His is a straightforward argument for a rejection of egalitarianism with a consequent return to rigorous basics.

Basic Knowledge

The last reform points out that we have drifted from requiring proficiency in certain basic subjects. For example, Diane Ravitch and Chester Finn conducted a study funded by the National Endowment for the Humanities that established what common sense tells us already—there is a connection between what is studied in school and what the students know and don't know. The debacle we call modern education is not resulting in an increase of *stupidity*; it is resulting in ignorance, which is another thing altogether. If no one teaches them, how can they know? In the published results of this study (*What Do Our 17-Year-Olds Know?*), these two researchers answer the question somewhat grimly. Our seventeen-year-olds don't know much.

Fewer than 60 percent of the students know, for example, that:
Tom Sawyer is famous for clever ways of getting out of trouble and work (59.8 percent).
Herman Melville and Joseph Conrad wrote novels about the sea (34.7 percent).
Pilgrim's Progress is an allegory about the temptations Christians face in life (13.4 percent).[43]

So much for literature. The results from history are not encouraging either.

In several other cases, the knowledge gaps are even more astonishing. One student in five (20.8 percent), for example, does not know that George Washington commanded the American army during the Revolution; almost one in three (32 percent) doesn't know that Lincoln wrote the Emancipation Proclamation. Nearly a quarter (22.6 percent) fail to name Richard Nixon as the president whose resignation resulted from Watergate.[44]

They conclude with a call for change in the content of what is taught. They do acknowledge that history and literature are not static, unchanging subjects. But they argue forcefully that there is a core of knowledge which all our students need and which few are getting. "This is a tall order. But we do not think it is an impossible order. Nor do we think it is beyond the capacity of our educating institutions. Certainly is is not beyond the capacities of our seventeen-year-olds."[45]

CHRISTIAN REFORM OF THE SCHOOLS

On the question of education, Christians appear to be split among three basic options. The first is to be "salt and light" within the public school system, which is our concern in this section. The second option is to establish and maintain private Christian schools, and the third is to teach children at home, both of which will be addressed in coming chapters.[46]

Fifty years ago, Christians who had their children in the public schools did not need to justify their actions to anyone. There was no apparent crisis in education, and public schools were for everyone. In fact, at one time evangelical Protestants thought of the public schools as being "theirs." But with the manifestation of overt humanism in the public schools and the response of a vigorous (and sometimes militant) private education movement, Christians who remain within the public system have begun to present their arguments for remaining.[47]

Christians who have not given up on the public schools have expended much energy in attempts at reform. The two most visible battles have been the effort to reinstate prayer in school and the attempt to have creation taught alongside evolution. In addition, these reformers have been concerned about things like anti-Christian bias in textbooks, immoral teaching in sex-ed classes, and so forth. They believe, rightly, that education cannot take place in a moral vacuum and that it needs to return to Judeo/Christian values.

The first task of such reformers is to demonstrate the problem, which isn't all that difficult. Paul Vitz, a professor of psychology at New York University, conducted a study of public school textbooks, clearly demonstrating that an anti-Christian bias exists. He said, "Those responsible for these books appear to have a deep-seated fear of any form of active contemporary Christianity, especially serious, committed Protestantism."[48] In the portion of the study dealing with social studies textbooks for grades one to four, Vitz found that "not one of the forty books totaling ten thousand pages had one text reference to a primary religious activity occurring in representative contemporary American life."[49] Vitz believes the problem is the result of top-heavy bureaucracy, the local educator's loss of authority, the anti-traditional values of the education leadership, and the radical agenda of the NEA.[50]

The bias against Christianity is not found only in textbooks for children; it can also be clearly seen in texts for teaching future teachers. In a textbook designed "particularly for classes in children's literature in English and education departments,"[51] the bias against Christian values is manifest. In a section entitled "The Puritans and Perdition," we learn this: "A group of deeply religious people whom we know as the Puritans read their Bibles with fervor. They venerated the victims of religious persecution and studied Foxe's *Book of Martyrs* (1563), with its details of death at the stake, and gave the book to their children. As if this legacy of terror was not enough for small Puritans to endure . . . "[52] We are instructed later that if a book is to be suitable for children, it must not be marred with any "moralizing."[53] We all know how kids hate moralizing.

There are some broader indications that criticisms such as Vitz offers are right on target and that some adjustments are being made. A recent headline in *The New York Times* ran, "Trend Gaining in

Public Schools to Add Teaching About Religion."[54] The story went on to cite new guidelines from the California Department of Education which say that "students must become familiar with the basic ideas of the major religions and ethical tradition of each time and place."[55] Two cheers? One?

At the very least, it is doubtful that this is genuine reform. It is much more likely a sop to the many Christians who are still in the schools, but who might take a walk if annoyed much further. An estimated 80 percent of evangelical Protestants are still committed in some way to the public school system.[56] For example, the four-teen-million-member Southern Baptist Convention is on record as supporting the public schools.[57] Given how much it has taken to make Christian parents unhappy with the schools, it probably wouldn't take much to pacify them again, and that is what I think we are seeing here.[58] The sort of "reform" that is going on has to do with teaching *about* various religions, including Christianity. But the foundation of such teaching is a commitment to a religion other than Christianity.

Still, Christians continue to agitate for changes in the public system. Ernest Boyer, president of the Carnegie Foundation for the Advancement of Teaching, argued in a recent article that moral reform in the public system is urgently needed. He says, "To have people who are well informed but not constrained by conscience is, conceivably, the most dangerous outcome of education possible. Indeed, it could be argued that ignorance is better than unguided intelligence, for the most dangerous people are those who have knowledge without a moral framework."[59]

Beyond this, others are not content just to argue *for* the positive presentation of traditional values. It is one thing to argue that the schools do not emphasize ethics enough; it is quite another to say that they are centers for the promulgation of immorality. For example, Gary Bauer, a former Under Secretary of Education, argues against "Values Clarification," which purports to be an objective and scientific way to enable students to think through ethical issues.

In one Values Clarification class, students congenially concluded that a fellow student would be foolish to return $1,000 she found in a purse at school. The teacher's reaction: "If I come from a position of what is right and wrong, then I am not their counselor."[60]

Bauer concludes, "Our goal in teaching values is not merely the transmission of a desired set of beliefs. Rather, it is a process, integrated into the general curriculum, which provides students with a clear articulation of the norms and concepts that have sustained this free and democratic society since its founding. . . ."[61]

In other words, what is needed is a return to traditional Judeo/Christian values. This means the anti-moral, anti-Christian bias in the public school system must be rejected. Jacqueline Kasun, a professor of economics at Humboldt State University, gives another example of this kind of amorality in teaching. She reports on a curriculum guide for a school in Ferndale, California, which "suggests that high school students work as boy-girl pairs on 'physiology definition sheets' in which they define 'foreplay,' 'erection,' 'ejaculation,' and similar terms. Whether or not students are satisfied with their 'size of sex organs' is suggested as a topic of class discussion in this curriculum."[62] John Whitehead, founder of the Rutherford Institute, observes, "The undermining of traditional family moral structures in public education has been both subtle and direct." He goes on to document practices which not only undermine the morality of the student, but also the integrity and privacy of his family.[63]

The solution to this kind of thing should be obvious, right? If the problem is caused by an abandonment of traditional values, then the solution would be to get those values back in the classroom. Unfortunately, it is easier to criticize such moral follies than to get the system to change. This is because there are many Americans who pay property taxes who do not hold to such "traditional values." It is true that the system is currently imposing on Christians who pay taxes, but is the solution to do the same thing to those who disagree with the Christians? If Christians are unsuccessful in getting such values back into the public schools, then they should not want their children exposed to such false teaching. But if they are successful, then haven't they wronged the humanists in the same way Christians have been wronged? The Bible tells us to return good for evil (Romans 12:17).

Another way to understand this is by means of the golden rule—do as you would be done by. I currently pay taxes to pay for the propagation of a religious faith I do not believe.[64] Although the Bible teaches that coercion and force are legitimate tools for the civil magistrate to use, there are limitations placed on the scope of that force (Romans 13:1-7). Requiring people to believe a certain way is not within the jurisdiction of the civil magistrate; it is immaterial whether the belief required is true or false. So if I object to paying taxes for this reason, then I should not turn around and do the same thing to someone else. To do so would not be charitable. So in this battle for the public schools, it is folly for the Christians to continue to lose and inconsistent for them to win.

One might reply that we live in a democracy and that Christians should work through democratic processes to restore traditional Judeo/Christian values to the public schools. The difficulty with this is the fact that it legitimizes humanist impositions on Christians as well. As long as 51 percent of those who vote agree with it, the tenets of one religion may be imposed on the adherents of another, with the bill paid by all. Christians, of all people, should recognize that might does not make right—even if it is a democratic might.[65]

IS SCHOOL PRAYER AN ANSWER?

The issue of prayer in the public schools illustrates this principle exactly. At the same time, because it is an emotional issue, the principle is almost never applied. The secularists don't apply it because to do so would require abandoning the pretense of neutrality which they have kept up for so long. The Christians don't apply it because they think the debate is over *prayer*.

Great battles are frequently fought over the meaning and treatment of symbols. One example was the reaction of the American public when the Supreme Court declared that burning the American flag was speech protected under the First Amendment. There was a great public outcry and controversy—all over a piece of cloth. In such controversies, sometimes there is an awareness of the underlying issues, and sometimes there is not.

Prayer in the public schools is a similar issue. On the surface it is easy to see how those concerned for traditional values would support a return to prayer in the public schools. After all, the reasoning goes, shouldn't we seek to halt the swelling tide of disrespect for those values? What better way to do this than by giving public school children the opportunity to pray? Wouldn't this have beneficial effects in the areas of discipline, respect for authority, and morality?

In 1962, the Supreme Court decided that school-sponsored prayer was unconstitutional. Since that time, many Christians have been in the forefront of the efforts to restore prayer to the public schools.[66] Their opponents have not been few, and arguments against school prayer have not been lacking. What has been lacking is an understanding that prayer in the public schools is something that Christians, *as Christians*, should strenuously oppose. The common belief that school prayer would help restore morality is based only on superficial reasoning.

There is an effective case to be made against secularism and the influence it has in the public school system. But to the extent Christians advocate school prayer, to that same extent they are tacitly granting legitimacy to what the secularists have done to them. If it is permissible to tax a secular humanist to support a school where prayer is officially encouraged, then why isn't it permissible to tax a Christian to support a school where blasphemy is officially encouraged? When public schools began, they were strongly influenced by evangelical Christians. Because they were state schools this meant that everyone (Jew, Catholic, etc.) had to help support a school system that was propagating a worldview they did not share. It should be obvious that such a system is not a just one.

When secularists took control of the schools, the more traditional expressions of religious belief, prayer included, were forced out. But when this happened, the secularists were only doing *what had previously been done to them*. They had learned their lesson well. This turn of events might have been anticipated. The United States was and is a pluralistic country. Because education cannot be neutral about certain basic issues (What is man? What is society? Where did we come from?) and because in a pluralistic society people disagree on such issues, it is impossible to impose state education on the entire society without putting these various groups into conflict. They struggle for control of the school system, and the group in control violates the religious liberties of the other groups. Currently, the secularists are violating the rights of believers, and the believers are seeking to overthrow the secularists. When they have done so, the secularists will be the ones whose liberties are being violated.

If the educational system refuses to address these basic issues, then it is refusing to educate. But if the questions are addressed, they will be addressed in the light of a certain worldview. Promoting a worldview can be done in public schools only if it is legitimate to violate the rights of the groups who do not agree and are not in control. The root problem is the imposition of state education in a pluralistic nation. In such a situation, conflict over the control of education is inevitable.[67]

We must also consider the nature of prayer. It is curious that Christians are pushing so strenuously for prayer which they don't believe to be prayer. Christians pray to the Father of the Lord Jesus Christ—not to Allah, Krishna, or God-as-you-conceive-him/her-to-be. If we were successful in establishing *Christian* prayer in the schools, we would be violating the religious liberties of those who are not Christians. If we establish prayer that is not Christian, what have we gained? Why fight to get prayer in the schools when you believe the prayers, once instituted, won't get past the ceiling? Do we really want our children led in a daily vain repetition?

Biblical prayer has to meet certain standards. It must not come from deceitful lips (Psalm 17:1); those who lift their hands to God must see to it that these are holy hands (1 Timothy 2:8). Prayer is part of a constant, ongoing devotion (Acts 1:14; 2:42; Colossians 4:2). The one who offers prayer to God should believe (Mark 11:24). God is pleased with prayer when it comes from someone who is righteous (Proverbs 15:8, 29; 1 Peter 3:12). In prayer we present our requests to God (Philippians 4:6), and from a righteous man, fervent prayer is powerful (James 5:16). Prayer should be offered in trust (1 Chronicles 5:20), thanksgiving (Ephesians 1:16), joy (Philippians 1:4), and in the Spirit (Ephesians 6:18). Christians pray to God the Father in the name of God the Son, motivated by God the Spirit (Ephesians 2:18). And if we neglect the law of God and attempt to pray, that prayer is an abomination (Proverbs 28:9).

If Christians object to secular humanism as an established non-Christian worldview in the schools, then it makes no sense to fight to establish *another* non-Christian worldview—worship of the God of the Lowest Common Denominator. If this problem is corrected by instituting Christian prayer, then we are back to our earlier unjust arrangement. Because our society is so diverse, there is no way to establish school prayer unless there is compromise on the content of prayer. In our society, individuals from a multitude of different religions, denominations, and worldviews are enrolled in the public schools. This means that any prayer acceptable to the majority of all these groups would have all the doctrinal rigor of oatmeal. Students would learn to pray to a mush god; the god of the civil religion. The various theologies of Mormons, Catholics, evangelicals, etc., would be run through a blender and the resulting concoction assembled into a prayer. Such prayers would be a theological monstrosity. If the secularists were included in the compromise (and to be fair, they must be), then the result will be, not a prayer, but a moment of silence[68] in which the students are allowed to pray, lust, blaspheme, or whatever else suits them.

THE DANGER OF REACTION

There is a vast difference between action and reaction. As Christians, we are called to principled obedience to the Word of God. We are not called to a reactionary faith. Reactionaries can only maintain, at best, a limited defensive position—as has been evident in the field of Christian education. In the past ten years, many thousands of Christian parents have removed their children from the public schools.[69] They have either begun to educate them at home or have placed them in private Christian schools.

This movement to private education has been praiseworthy in many respects. But one unfortunate aspect is that it has been largely reactionary, a response to various problems: the prohibition of school prayer, rampant drug use, sexual immorality, lack of discipline, declining academic standards and test scores, etc. All these things are matters of concern to Christians—but Christians should not *react* to them. Our opposition must be principled, and the principles must be based on the clear teaching of Scripture. If we allow ourselves to become reactionaries for Christ, then we will find ourselves in a pitched battle against mere symptoms. Instead, as thinking Christians, we should seek to understand the worldview that has produced these symptoms in the public school system, and we should do battle with *that*.

In the late nineteenth century, long before all these symptoms appeared, R. L. Dabney, a prophetic theologian, predicted the complete secularization of public education in America. His prediction was based on principle and has come to pass with depressing accuracy. He said, "Christians must prepare themselves then, for the following results: All prayers, catechisms, and Bibles will ultimately be driven out of the schools."[70] How could he have known this when he did? The answer is that he had a Biblical worldview, which he applied to the question of education in a pluralistic America.

In contrast, much in the modern Christian school movement has developed in reaction to what is wrong in public education. The fruit of secular, humanistic education is clearly seen for what it is, and it is rejected. This is a good start, but it is not enough to fight a rear-guard action against humanism. We must go on and develop a Biblical vision for the education of our children. Until this is done, the Christian school movement will not have the impact it could have. The Christian "reaction" in the last ten years has had a substantial impact. But a principled assumption of responsibility on the part of Christian parents would have an enormous effect—far beyond anything we have seen up to this point.

CONCLUSION

Many of the reforms listed in this chapter are hard to quarrel with. If there is any hope for public education in America at all, some genuine reforms must be implemented, and quickly. After the education summit, former Secretary of Education William Bennett said that we had little time to turn things around. He said, "I'd give the education reform movement another five years. If we're not able to get our schools back to where they were in 1963, after spending 40 percent more, then maybe we should just declare bankruptcy, give the people back their money, and let them start their own schools. That would be a radical way to have accountability."[71]

Time *is* short. If only half of these reformers are right, we have a monumental task in front of us and very little time to accomplish it. But before we join the chorus of voices calling for reform, there is one other issue to consider, which will be addressed in the coming chapters. Is it possible that these reformers, while insightful on many issues, have failed to take the importance of *foundations* into account? Is the house falling because it is built on sand?

PART TWO

AN APPROACH TO DISTINCTIVELY CHRISTIAN EDUCATION

THREE

THE TRUE MINISTRY OF EDUCATION

THE ROLE OF THE FAMILY

God has instituted various governments among men, and one is the government of the family. It is in the family that fundamental decisions about the education and training of children are made or not made. Most Christian parents provide the children instruction in the faith one day a week at church and at Sunday school. Many families also instruct the children at home during a daily devotional time.[1] This is good, but it is not enough by itself. Unfortunately, some Christian parents feel they have met their obligation to educate their children if they simply send them off to public school, provided they also go to Sunday school. *All* the instruction received by the children should be permeated with God's Word. Consider this passage from Deuteronomy on education:

> Hear, O Israel: The Lord our God, the Lord is one. Love the Lord your God with all your heart and with all your soul and with all your strength. These commandments that I give you today are to be upon your hearts. Impress them on your children. Talk about them when you sit at home and when you walk along the road, when you lie down and when you get up. Tie them as symbols on your hands and bind them on your foreheads. Write them on the door frames of your houses and on your gates (Deuteronomy 6:4-9).

The same mentality about education can be seen in the New Testament: "Children, obey your parents in the Lord, for this is right. 'Honor your father and mother,' which is the first commandment with a promise—'that it may go well with you and that you may enjoy long life on the earth.' Fathers, do not exasperate your children; instead, bring them up in the training and instruction of the Lord" (Ephesians 6:1-4).

Christian parents must take into account three things as they consider their obligation to educate their children. The first is the instruction that children should live in an environment dominated by Scripture. We must not dismiss such passages as pertaining only to a simple agrarian culture. If life in the latter half of the twentieth century is more complex, it does not follow that we have *less* need for instruction in the law of God![2] If God wanted children then to think about everything in the light of His Word, then this practice is certainly as necessary now. In a more complex society, there is more to think about. Obviously, instruction on Sunday only is not enough. A thorough Biblical instruction can only be provided when related to all of life. Teaching must occur when we walk, drive, sit, and lie down. Nothing can be clearer—God wants the children of His people to *live* in an environment conditioned by His Word. Parents who want their children to be equipped to face the world that will exist twenty years from now will need to give this kind of comprehensive instruction in God's words.

In our family, we have done many things to maintain this kind of environment. Our son has listened to hours of Bible tapes as he has drifted off to sleep. We have sung hymns in the car as we traveled. We have had vigorous dinner table discussions of various theological issues. As our children were learning to talk, I would teach them a word (say, *moon*), and then I asked them, "Who made the moon?" "God!" God's Word should not be limited to "devotions." And as our children go off to school, we are grateful that their formal education reinforces what we do as a family.

The second thing we must remember is that we are commanded to love the Lord our God with *all* our *minds* (Matthew 22:37). The command to teach children all the time is not limited to *religious* instruction. If our children do not think like Christians when they study history, math, or science, then they are not obeying the command to love God with *all* their minds. And if they are not obeying the command, parents should ask themselves why they are not. It is also noteworthy that Jesus taught us that this is the greatest command. Many Christians know that the greatest command requires love, but love to them is nothing more than a vague and undefined benevolence. According to the command, whom do we love? With what means are we to love Him? It is clear that God's people, and their children, are required to love the Lord their God with all their *brains*.

This involves more than a short lesson once a week; it involves more than a general acquaintance with David, Goliath, Samson, Noah, et al. What we must strive for is an education involving every aspect of the child's life. The child must be taught how to love the Lord God with all the mind. If parents fail at this, a child may pick up a non-Biblical worldview from someone else. At some point, the child will see the conflict between the two views and reject one teaching and accept the other, or he will become intellectually schizophrenic in his worldview. He will throw a little switch in his mind when he goes to church and he will believe *this*, and when he goes back to the office or to the college classroom, he will flip another switch in order to believe *that*. This comes from failing to receive a comprehensive education.[3]

Now when the conflict between Christianity and secularism becomes apparent, not all children will reject the faith of their parents (although most either reject it or become intellectually confused). In some cases, Christian parents may effectively neutralize the impact of a public school education on their children. Faced with conflicting views, children decide to believe what they learned at home. When they are young, children can be incredibly loyal. My youngest daughter asks me which team I want to win the game or which candidate I support in an election. Then she announces, "I'm going for him too!" This loyalty can be cultivated and maintained throughout the educational process.

That is what happened to me. I got a public school education all the way through my Master's degree, and I rejected much erroneous teaching along the way. My parents' teaching at home had made a major impact on me. Our family would debate various issues around the dinner table, and independence of mind (within a Biblical framework) was strongly encouraged. And it is quite true that I went through the secular system and survived. But have our expectations for education fallen so far that we are now excited when our children *survive* it?

Unfortunately, many parents do not have this kind of impact on their children. The secularism is not being effectively neutralized at home. When the children are grown, they bow down to other gods—or they stay with the faith of their fathers on Sunday and the faith of the secularists the rest of the week.

God has given parents a profound authority over children. If they use that authority correctly, with much love and affection, the children will wholeheartedly follow the God of their parents. In Ephesians, fathers are told to bring their children up in the training and instruction of the Lord. In Timothy and Titus, the elders of the church are required to manage their households well. In Titus, the elders are required to have children who are *believers*—which implies that fathers can bring their children to belief.

In Deuteronomy 6:1-2, we are told the commands of the Lord are to be observed so that "you, your children and their children" may fear the Lord your God. In the Decalogue (Deuteronomy 5:9), we are commanded with regard to idols, ". . . you shall not bow down to them or worship them; for I, the Lord your God, am a jealous God, punishing the children for the sin of the fathers to the third and fourth generation of those who hate me, but showing love to a thousand generations of those who love me and keep my commandments." The sins of fathers are visited to the third and fourth generations, but the righteousness of fathers is visited to thousands of generations. The promise of blessing is a stronger promise.

One time my youngest daughter was sitting on my lap telling me about the death of Jesus on the cross. She was probably three or four at the time. It struck me with some force that there wasn't a doctrine in her head that we hadn't put there. She was reciting it back to us with great authority and confidence. What also struck me was that this is how the system was *designed* to work. God didn't choose that humans be born as mature people—the better able to search for truth autonomously. He put children in their parents' charge, and then He instructed the parents to teach their children in a certain way. A child *should* come to belief on the authority of the parents.[4] This is how God designed the family, and this is also why it is such a grievous sin when a parent abuses this position of authority.

Does this mean a child has no means of verifying the truth? Not at all. We tell our children all about a God of love who sent His Son to die for His people. As we teach, we should be adequately demonstrating that same love to them. This provides them with epistemological verification, although the child obviously would not put it this way. The child learns that what his parents teach is internally consistent. Even a young child knows whether there is consistency between what is being said and what is being lived. If orthodox parents teach the children correct doctrine but mistreat them, are the children going to grow up to be godly? In the goodness and mercy of God, it is possible, but unlikely. If it does happen, it will be in spite of the parental hypocrisy.

Not only are parents responsible to oversee the Biblical teaching of their children, they are also responsible to see that their children don't receive false teaching.[5] Error is pervasive. It can come from TV, from library books, or from peers, as well as from school.[6] A Christian parent has two options. The first is to neutralize the false teaching, which means the parents have to spend at least a few hours every night countering what the children learned in school. This is difficult because the parents don't know exactly what the children learned that day. The children are not yet trained to come back and report on what was unbiblical in what they heard. Responsible oversight is extremely difficult.[7]

The second option is a private school (home schooling as one form of private schooling will be dealt with in a separate chapter). In this situation, it is *possible* for parents who take their responsibility seriously to do a good job. But there is a temptation for Christian parents to use private schools as an abdication of responsibility, albeit an abdication about which they can feel good. At Logos, we have many parents who take their responsibility for educating their children very seriously indeed. But sadly, we also have parents who give us nothing more than their children and the tuition money.

In contrast, parents *should* see the work of the Christian school as a supplement to their own teaching, enabling the parents to be even more effective in *their* time with their children. The *parents* are the ones given the charge to educate, train, and instruct their children. That responsibility cannot be handed over to an institution. The Christian school has no more business usurping the authority of parents than does the state. This sort of abdication has already happened with some Sunday school programs, and tragically, there are some who are beginning to treat the Christian school the same way.

Should we send our children to Sunday school or to a Christian school so that *we* won't have to instruct them? Nothing could be further from the instruction of Deuteronomy—we are to teach our children when we sit down, when we drive, and when we eat meals together. We cannot abdicate *our* responsibility by assigning it to someone else (including a Christian school). God is going to hold us accountable for what our children learn, whether or not we were the ones who taught them. It all comes back to parental responsibility, which cannot be taken for granted.

STATE INDOCTRINATION NETWORK: SIN?

Tony Campolo, a well-known Christian speaker and writer, calls the question of whether Christians should have their children in the public schools a "hot potato."[8] He says further, treating it as a hot potato himself, that the answer to the question is, "it all depends." Another Christian writer, Robert Thoburn, says that the church "should begin to examine members who are sending their children to public schools. Pressure should be placed on them by the elders . . . [who] should limit voting members to those who refuse to send their dependent children to public schools."[9] Someone else has said that the public schools should be considered the State Indoctrination Network: SIN.[10]

How are Christian parents to handle this question? Is it a "sin" to send your children to public schools? There is certainly disagreement in the broad Christian community on the question. Still the fact of the disagreement tells us nothing in itself. It is possible for Christians to disagree among themselves; this does not necessarily mean that the teaching of the Bible is unclear. A simplistic, cursory exegesis is unlikely to discover what the Bible clearly teaches.

Christians can begin by assuming that there is no area of life where Biblical principles are irrelevant. (This is the assumption upon which the entire Turning Point Christian Worldview Series is based.) So even though the Bible does not directly address every problem in the modern world by name, Biblical principles can be brought to bear on *every* problem. This certainly includes the question of how God wants children reared. As Christian parents work through this issue, I believe there are certain key principles which must be kept in mind.

Difficult Cases

Difficult cases make bad law. If I have to step out of the classroom for a moment, I may tell the students they are required to stay in their seats. I have noticed that when I do so, students tend to think immediately of extraordinary circumstances which would justify them in disregarding the requirement. "But, Mr. Wilson, what if there is a fire drill?" Or "What if the school is hit by a meteor?" This tendency is seen on a trivial level in the classroom, and it is seen on a monumental scale with issues such as abortion. A handful of "difficult cases" (in which the mother will lose her life, for example) is used to justify a million and a half convenience abortions a year.

The same thing occurs in discussions about public education.

I believe a solid case can be made for the necessity of Christian education, but that case will not be heard if we spend our time talking about a working woman with a quadriplegic husband and five kids, with the nearest Christian school located two hundred miles away. Nor can we keep bringing up those Christians who live in an area where public education is far less hostile to Christianity than most public schools. Their oasis should not be the basis for understanding the "big picture" concerning public education. And besides, the "oasis" may have far less water in it than the residents have been led to believe. The case should be decided on Biblical principle, and then we should decide what to do for those who would have difficulty applying the principle.

Double Standards

Using double standards for evaluating educational systems must be avoided. I have noticed a tendency for some Christian parents to be intolerant of relatively trivial problems in a Christian school, and then when they have placed their children in the public school, they tolerate the serious educational and ethical breakdown. For example, a junior high student may be pulled out of a Christian school because there are not enough social activities, or the sports program is not adequate. The child is then placed in a school where social activities are plentiful, but so are drugs and alcohol, along with rampant sexual immorality.

It reminds me of a problem Paul had at Corinth. "In fact, you even put up with anyone who enslaves you or exploits you or takes advantage of you or pushes himself forward or slaps you in the face. To my shame I admit that we were too weak for that!" (2 Corinthians 11:20-21). The Corinthians would tolerate in false teachers much more than they would accept from an apostle. Public schools and Christian schools must both be measured by the same standard—the Word of God. The tendency is to hold Christian schools to a strict standard because they are Christian (which is good), but then to drastically lower expectations for the public schools because there is no profession of Christianity. But we should not grade the various school systems "on a curve." We should hold all forms of education up against the same Biblical standard and then make our decision.

Experience

Experiences—good or bad—are not to be the basis of any decision. I regard my public education experience as a sort of "best-case scenario." I was educated in the public school system, and I grew up in a godly Christian home. I know firsthand that it is possible for Christian kids to make it through the public system without losing their faith. I did not lose mine, nor did my brothers and sister. But should survival be the goal of education? Survival is one thing, and a godly education is quite another.

Whenever I was conscious of conflict between what I learned at school and what I learned at home, there was no problem. I believed what my parents taught me. There were times when the conflict was obvious. In high school, my class was once told that all teens go through a time when they hate their parents, and that it was all right. I knew better. But as I have grown in my adult understanding of the Christian faith, I have become increasingly aware of conflicts I did not recognize as a child—conflicts at the level of presuppositions. I have had to unlearn many things, and I have no desire for my children to go through the same process.

In the same way, people who have had bad experiences in the public school system should not make that the basis of their actions. Reactionary support for Christian education is not helpful in the long run. Parents should always proceed on the basis of what they believe to be the teaching of the Scripture.

Social Adjustment

The response of peers and the school system to a godly student should be anticipated. Parents who send their kids to the public school frequently do so in order to round out their social lives. Christian schools are usually smaller and cannot compete with public schools in athletics, band, dances, and so forth. But the parents of these kids also want them to stay out of compromising situations. These two desires are often inconsistent. For example, the chances are excellent that if a teenager lived a consistent Christian life at the high school, he would be respected—and isolated. Frequently, the ticket to popularity is called compromise. So if the goal is "friends," the parents should read the price tag. In other words, if the social goal is reached, it may involve compromise, and if there is no compromise, then the social goals may be sacrificed. On this point, I speak from personal experience. I tried to be a consistent Christian in the high school I attended, and I know how lonely it can be.

Many Christian parents do not expect the general population of the public schools to have the same standard of morality they do. The parents conclude that Christian kids should attend the public schools in order to be "salt and light." Parents need to ask whether, taken as a whole, Christian kids *are* being salt and light. There are millions of professing evangelical Christians in America today, and many of their children are in the public schools. Do they make a difference? One of our recent graduates who decided to come to Logos School did so in part because the Christian students at the public school she attended were not all that different from the rest of the students. It is one thing to be a "Christian" at church and quite another to act like a Christian when a price tag is attached.

Is this a fair evaluation? Are the children from Christian families the testimony their parents and pastors desire them to be? Or do they go with the flow? Josh McDowell has recently released a study that shows that the sexual behavior of children from evangelical homes is not appreciably different from that of their secular counterparts. He reports that by age eighteen, 43 percent of churched youth have had sexual intercourse.[11] From my own experience as a pastor, I know the problems in this area are severe. I believe we would be hard pressed to show that Christian kids are making a major difference in the public schools.

Although there is no "sin" called "sending kids to public school," the moral responsibilities of parents with regard to education are considerable. These responsibilities include providing a godly environment for instruction, teaching children to obey the first commandment by loving God with all their *minds*, evaluating Christian and secular school systems by the same standard, and recognizing the destructive impact a secular school system would have on their children. These considerations, taken together, do indicate that a good Christian education is a moral necessity.

F O U R

THE NATURE OF KNOWLEDGE

THE NONALIGNMENT MYTH

One of the great ironies among modern evangelicals is the fact that many have higher and stricter standards for their children's baby-sitters than they do for their children's teachers. Is a baby-sitter needed? She should be a Christian, and a reliable one. She should be known to the family, or highly recommended by someone who is. And for what task? To keep Johnny safe and dry until bedtime and then to tuck him in.

But five years later, Johnny comes home from his first day of school. He bursts in the front door, full of news. His parents ask all kinds of questions. And one of them is: "Who is your teacher, Johnny?" The parents don't know the teacher's name. They don't know if the teacher is an atheist or a Southern Baptist. They don't know if he is a socialist or a conservative Republican. They don't know if she is lesbian or straight. And what is the teacher's task? Her task is to help them shape the way the child thinks about the world. Does God exist? If He exists, is His existence *relevant* to the classroom? And what is the nature of man? What is the purpose of society? How did man get here? Where should he go? How should he conduct himself on the way? None of these questions can be answered without certain worldview assumptions, and the parents in this example do not even know whether they share the worldview of their child's teacher.

There are two reasons why many parents have allowed this to

happen. The first is that the government has become the guarantor of "quality" in teaching. If something is "licensed" or "accredited," one assumes the quality is good. We forget that licensing also means control. The government has not yet taken on a licensing role with regard to baby-sitting or parenting; when it does, no doubt some will acquiesce. But God has assigned the responsibility, and to shift it elsewhere for the sake of "quality-control" is abdication. The second reason is related to the first. Neutrality is impossible; worldviews in education are unavoidable. Jesus eliminated neutrality in all areas when He said, "He who is not with me is against me, and he who does not gather with me scatters " (Matthew 12:30).

About a century before anyone was listening, R. L. Dabney described the impossibility of neutrality in education this way:

> The instructor has to teach history, cosmogony, psychology, ethics, the laws of nations. How can he do it without saying anything favorable or unfavorable about the beliefs of evangelical Christians, Catholics, Socinians, Deists, pantheists, materialists, or fetish worshippers, who all claim equal rights under American institutions? His teaching will indeed be "the play of Hamlet, with the part of Hamlet omitted."[1]

Concerning the question of origins, he asked if a scientist could give the ". . . genesis of earth and man, without indicating whether Moses or Huxley is his prophet?"[2] The answer of course is that directionless, nonaligned education is by definition impossible. Certain worldview assumptions must always be made. They will either be based on Biblical truth, or they will not. There is no neutrality. A bumper sticker says, "Everybody has got to be somewhere!" Applied to geographical location, the statement is a tautological joke. But if we apply it to worldviews in education, we have a profound truth—so profound that many miss it. Children are taught by missionaries of a rival faith, and some parents continue to slumber.

I once gave a presentation on Christian education to a group of parents. One of the parents took strong exception to the position I presented and told how she had communicated her feelings about the celebration of Halloween at the public school where her child attended. She apparently considered this to be evidence that Christian parents can make a difference in the public schools. While many are certainly trying, I feel the effort is misguided. Such attempts at "reform" are usually unsuccessful and are a good modern example of straining at gnats and swallowing camels. Does it make sense to object to the *inclusion* of witches and goblins one day a year and not object to the *exclusion* of God the rest of the year?

THE DIFFERENCE GOD MAKES

I was once instructing our seventh grade Bible class when one of the boys interrupted me with, "But that's a universal statement!" It turns out that in the previous science class the students had been taught about universal statements, and this student regarded with suspicion the appearance of one in Bible class. He was attempting to apply in one class what he had learned in another. I answered the objection in class, but when the class was over, I took the student aside and praised him for attempting the application. Obviously, educators want to get the students to think in class. But the real goal should be to get them to think in the hallways *between* classes.

God is the Light in which we see and understand everything else. Without Him, the universe is a fragmented pile of incomprehensible particulars. Indeed, the universe can no longer be understood as a universe; it has become a multiverse. Christian education must therefore present all subjects as parts of an integrated whole with the Scriptures at the center. Without this integration, the curriculum will be nothing more than a dumping ground for unrelated facts. When God is acknowledged, all knowledge coheres. It is obvious that all aspects of this coherence cannot be known to us—we are finite creatures. But as the late Francis Schaeffer would put it, while our knowledge cannot be exhaustive, we can grasp what is true. We can understand that God knows what we do not, and therefore the universe is unified *in principle*. Where God is not acknowledged, the pursuit of knowledge is just one thing after another and the ultimate exercise in futility. The French existentialist philosopher Sartre understood this when he said that without an infinite reference point, all finite points are absurd.

Education is a completely religious endeavor. It is impossible to impart knowledge to students without building on religious presuppositions. Education is built on the foundation of the instructor's worldview (and the worldview of those who developed the curriculum). It is a myth that education can be nonreligious—that is, that education can go on in a vacuum that deliberately excludes the basic questions about life. It is not possible to separate religious values from education. This is because all the fundamental questions of education require religious answers. Learning to read and write is simply the process of acquiring tools to enable us to ask and answer such questions.

Public education can approach this problem in one of two ways. The first is to refuse to address such questions. We have already seen that such an attempt is impossible. If any information is transferred at all, it will assume the truth of certain presuppositions. Every subject, every truth, bears some relationship to God. Every subject will be taught from a standpoint of submission or hostility to Him. The second alternative is the hidden agenda. The agenda is implemented when the state gives religious answers to the fundamental questions but hides the fact that it is doing so.[3] The religion is humanistic, and it is taught with the power of the state behind it. Thus, a church has been established by law, but it is not a Christian church. Without realizing it, many Christian parents are requiring their children to attend.

In contrast to this, the Apostle Paul teaches us that every thought is to be made captive to Christ (2 Corinthians 10:4-5). But how is this to be done, and how is this discipline of mind to be passed on to our children? There is no way to do it without a total teaching environment in submission to the Word of God. We cannot bring every thought captive by allowing some thoughts to aspire to autonomy. There is so much to learn about the Biblical worldview that it is impossible to accomplish it with Sunday school once a week, or even with daily devotional instruction in the home. Such daily instruction is rare to begin with, and even where it does exist, it is not possible to undo in such a short time (fifteen minutes? one hour?) what took many hours to do earlier that day.

PIOUS PROPAGANDA?

Teaching students to think in terms of a fixed reference point is not the same thing as indoctrination. It is more than devout propaganda. I was once speaking to a journalism class at Washington State University when one of the students asked rather pointedly whether Christian education was anything more than fundamentalist brainwashing. He didn't use those words, but the point was clear. I answered him by using the creation/evolution controversy as an example. I pointed out that the only school in our town where a student could receive accurate information about *both* sides of the debate was our school. Students in the public schools are not taught what creationists believe or what their supporting arguments are.

It is true that at Logos School, as in most Christian schools, we teach that creation is a fact. But it is that fixed reference point that enables us to present the arguments of our opponents as accurately as we can. We believe the Christian position can be honestly defended and are not afraid to let our students hear what the other side has to say. For example, our science teacher once brought in a professor from the University of Idaho and gave him two class periods to present the arguments for evolution to our ninth grade science class. A fixed reference point does not blind Christians to the existence of objections; it enables Christians to answer them.

I also pointed out to my questioner that in our Bible classes the students frequently challenge or question the Christian faith. This happens regularly, and when it does, the students are encouraged and their questions are answered. As iron sharpens iron, so students and teachers sharpen one another (Proverbs 27:17). The students are taught to think in terms of the Christian faith. This is what makes it possible for them to *think at all*. It is not propagandizing when teachers give their students a place to stand. Relativism has only the appearance of openness; in the end, it always frustrates the one who wants to acquire knowledge.

Some who realize how the public schools are failing do not recognize that the ultimate cause of the failure is theological; they dismiss Christian education as mere indoctrination. One example is Richard Mitchell, previously cited as a trenchant and hilarious critic of what passes for education in the public schools today. In spite of his opposition to the type of "education" provided by government schools, Mitchell refuses to regard private Christian schools as a legitimate alternative. He admits they do a better job teaching the "basics," and yet he opposes their commitment to "a certain ideology." In his words, "No school governed by ideology—any ideology whatsoever—can afford to educate its students; it can only indoctrinate and train them. In this respect there is no important difference between the 'Christian' schools and the government's schools. . . ."[4]

Later he defines the fruit of education as "a mind raised up in the habit of literacy and skill (it is one and the same thing) of language and thought."[5] But from a Biblical perspective, this sort of definition is inadequate; what good does it do to advocate training in thought and then neglect the role of thought? As the open mouth receives food, so the open, reasoning mind should close on truth. In a world without truth, skill in thinking is a useless skill. What good is thirst without water or hunger without food? In the same way, reasoning skills must lead to truth. Now it is true that some who claim to hold to Christian truth are unreasoning ideologues. But to argue from that fact to the position that all commitment to truth (by schools or individuals) must be unreasoning ideology is to be guilty of a *non sequitur* of the first rank. One could similarly argue that because counterfeit money exists, real money does not. As Samuel Rutherford used to say, "It followeth no way."[6]

Christians believe that Christ has been given a name that is above every name. "He is before all things, and in him all things hold together. And he is the head of the body, the church; he is the beginning and the firstborn from among the dead, so that in everything he might have the supremacy" (Colossians 1:17-18).

> It is this King, who, in the New Testament, is the God and Father of Jesus Christ, who directs and guides all things toward the *telos* which he has determined for creation. And this *telos* is the uniting of all things in Jesus Christ, "things in heaven and things on earth." (Ephesians 1:10; *see also* Romans 8:18-25; 11:36)[7]

We are not to limit the light of Christ to our understanding of *Christ*. We must understand the world in the light of Christ; He is the light in which we see truth. Christians cannot understand the world in a Biblical way without reference to Jesus Christ. In *Him* all things hold together (Colossians 1:15-18). Without this understanding, "Christian education" is no longer *Christ*ian; it is little more than baptized secularism. It is not enough to take the curricula of the government schools, add prayer and a Bible class, and claim the result is somehow Christian.

Humanistic education seeks to make man the defining principle for all knowledge. But man is too weak a glue to hold everything together. In himself he cannot provide this integrating principle. In contrast, educators who are truly Christian understand that Christ should be acknowledged as having the supremacy. This means that every fact, every truth, must be understood in that light. History, art, music, mathematics, etc., must all be taught in the light of God's existence and His revelation of Himself in His Son, Jesus Christ. Because the Scriptures occupy a central place in this revelation, they must also occupy a critical role in Christian education.

This is not to say the Bible was meant to be read as a science or mathematics text.[8] It was not. It does, however, provide a framework for understanding these so-called "secular" subjects. Without such a framework for understanding, all subjects will ultimately degenerate into chaotic absurdity—with each subject a pile of facts unto itself.[9] Again, Dabney: "Every line of true knowledge must find its completeness as it converges on God, just as every beam of daylight leads the eye to the sun. If religion is excluded from our study, every process of thought will be arrested before it reaches its proper goal. The structure of thought must remain a truncated cone, with its proper apex lacking."[10]

The Christian educator's job is not to require the students to spend all their time gazing at the sun. Rather, we want them to examine everything else in the light the sun provides. It would be utmost folly to try to blacken the sun in order to be able to study the world around us "objectively." Because all truth comes from God, the universe is coherent. Without God, particulars have no relationship to other particulars. Each subject has no relationship to any other subject. Christian educators must reject this understanding of the universe as a multiverse; the world is more than an infinite array of absurd "facts." The fragmentation of knowledge must therefore be avoided. History bears a relation to English, and biology a relation to philosophy; they all unite in the queen of the sciences, theology.[11]

J. Gresham Machen, a leader in the fight against theological liberalism earlier this century, stated it this way: "It is this profound Christian permeation of every human activity, no matter how secular the world may regard it as being, which is brought about by the Christian school and the Christian school alone."[12] This is a strong claim, but Machen goes on to back it up. "A Christian boy or girl can learn mathematics, for example, from a teacher who is not a Christian; and truth is truth however learned. But while truth is truth however learned, the bearing of truth, the meaning of truth, the purpose of truth, even in the sphere of mathematics, seem entirely different to the Christian from that which they seem to the non-Christian; and that is why a truly Christian education is possible only when Christian conviction underlies not a part, but all, of the curriculum of the school."[13]

Because truth is truth however learned, it is possible to teach students to balance their checkbooks without any reference to God. But this is not education; it is merely mental dexterity. Students are not being taught to think *thoroughly*. They are merely being trained to function in a particular way. When a student is taught to *think*, he or she will relate what is learned in one class to the information offered in another. But students can only do this when they have an integrating principle—something that will tie all the subjects together.

TROUSERED APES

C. S. Lewis wrote a provocative analysis of modern education entitled *The Abolition of Man: Reflections on Education with Special*

Reference to the Teaching of English in the Upper Forms of Schools.
In the book, Lewis argues that what occurs in elementary instruction has a profound impact, whether or not that impact is recognized. He begins the book thus: "I doubt whether we are sufficiently attentive to the importance of elementary textbooks."[14] Many Christians today would agree with his statement, but only because their children are being washed away in a flood of humanistic, anti-Biblical teaching.[15] When Lewis made the point, that flood was only a cloud the size of a man's fist.

It is a mistake to assume that the unbiblical nature of the curriculum must be *overt* before Christians oppose it. If we come to understand that a man's life is unified in his theology, whatever that theology is, then we will not be surprised to see what he affirms in one area surface in another. Lewis describes the power of the textbook writers, which "depends on the fact that they are dealing with a boy: a boy who thinks he is 'doing' his 'English prep' and has no notion that ethics, theology, and politics are all at stake. It is not a theory they put into his mind, but an assumption, which ten years hence, its origin forgotten and its presence unconscious, will condition him to take one side in a controversy which he has never recognized as a controversy at all."[16] In other words, implicit assumptions picked up in English have an effect, years later, in a completely different area. The result will ultimately be "trousered apes," as Lewis puts it—men who look like men, but who have been robbed of an important part of their humanity. This is because God made the world, and men must have a unifying principle even if their theology denies that one exists. Men must live as God made them, and not as they believe themselves to have evolved. Those with a fragmented worldview do not live in a vacuum; rather, from God they have their being (Acts 17:28). Because they deny Him, their application of any unifying principle must be inconsistent and a cause of constant philosophical frustration. Nevertheless, what is learned is still applied, and the subjectivist assumption picked up as a child in English has its destructive effect.

And what was it that alarmed Lewis about the direction education was taking? His critique was prompted by two textbook writers who had recounted the story of Coleridge at the waterfall. Coleridge had overheard two tourists respond in two different ways; he had mentally applauded the one who said the waterfall was "sublime" and rejected with disgust the response of the other, who said it was "pretty." To this, the textbook writers commented, in contrast to Coleridge, that when we say something is sublime, we are saying nothing more than that we have sublime feelings. "We appear to be saying something very important about something; and actually we are only saying something about our own feelings."[17] Lewis describes what is happening here as "momentous" and thought the error of such subjectivism important enough to dedicate a book to the subject.

In his response to another textbook writer, Lewis warns also about hidden agendas. "That is their day's lesson in English, though of English they have learned nothing. Another little portion of the human heritage has been quietly taken from them before they were old enough to understand."[18] Richard Weaver, who taught English at the University of Chicago, also taught us that ideas have consequences.[19] We see now that because ideas are interrelated, they can have consequences in the most unexpected places.

OUR GOLDEN CALVES

In considering the necessity of a Biblical integrating principle, there is an instructive passage in 1 Kings 12. The nation of Israel had split into two kingdoms, Judah and Israel. The king of Israel, Jeroboam, was concerned that if his people continued to travel south to Jerusalem to worship at the Temple, then their loyalty would ultimately revert to the king of Judah.

> Jeroboam thought to himself, "The kingdom will now likely revert to the house of David. If these people go up to offer sacrifices at the temple of the Lord in Jerusalem, they will again give their allegiance to their lord, Rehoboam king of Judah, and they will kill me and go back to Rehoboam king of Judah. They will kill me and return to King Rehoboam." After seeking advice, the king made two golden calves. He said to the people, "It is too much for you to go up to Jerusalem. Here are your gods, O Israel, who brought you up out of Egypt." One he set up in Bethel, and the other in Dan. And this thing became a sin; the people went even as far as Dan to worship the one there. (1 Kings 12: 26-30)

Thousands of years before George Orwell, Jeroboam discovered the memory hole. If the facts of history conflict with the current agenda, then so much the worse for the facts of history. Jehovah God brought Israel out of Egypt with an outstretched arm. This historical fact was inconvenient for Jeroboam. The solution? Make some golden calves and *rewrite the history curriculum*. Notice, however, that this rewriting depends upon something else for its success. It depends upon ignorance among the people of what really happened. Jeroboam can get away with his lie because the people have not been taught the truth. But in what area is their understanding of the truth lacking?

The people were being enticed into idolatry. The application of the lie was in the field of religion and theology. They were being taught to bow down in worship to golden calves. But the refutation of this lie was *in the field of history.* "What really happened when our fathers came out of Egypt, and how do we know?" In order for the people to resist the lie, they had to understand that different fields of knowledge are connected and that the connection was in the God of Abraham. Does history have a theological meaning? Is there any purpose to it? Do Christians believe that God acts in history?[20] A little closer to home, are there any facts in American history that are inconvenient to our modern Jeroboams? When America was founded, it was a Christian republic.[21] This historical fact is not widely accepted.[22] Does it make any difference whether Jeroboam or Moses writes the curriculum? Does it make any difference whether the teacher tells our children that Jerusalem is too far away and that *these* are the gods who delivered us?

Suppose for a moment in ancient Israel there was a school run by the priests who served these golden calves. Suppose further that some Israelite worshipers of the true God thought that it would be possible to send their children there to receive a "neutral" education, and they would then "unteach" whatever bad doctrine came with it. This approach reveals an attitude that either trivializes the difference God makes or overestimates its own ability to undo the damage.

Now the critic may feel that this skirts the issue. "Yes, yes," he says, "I believe that every thought should be made captive to Christ, but I do not believe $2 + 2 = 4$ to be part of the conflict between light and darkness. What difference could it make who teaches neutral subjects like mathematics? $2 + 2 = 4$ is true whether you are a Christian or a humanist." Not quite. Even here the impossibility of neutrality can be clearly seen. How do we know that $2 + 2 = 4$? Are we empiricists or rationalists? Are 2 and 4 mere linguistic conventions? Is our knowledge *a priori* or *a posteriori*? Do we remember this information from a previous life as Socrates taught? Is there any epistemological foundation for mathematics?[23]

On a more practical level, should a teacher of young children drill them in their math tables, or should she simply seek to get them to understand the concept? Do these different teaching methodologies reflect differences in worldview? The answer is: they certainly do. At Logos, we require that the children memorize quite a bit of material, and that involves work—productive work with lasting value. We require this because of our Biblical view of work. I have seen one result of this type of hard work around our dinner table. My children can beat me in answering questions such as, "What is 8 times 7?" They have memorized their tables and I didn't! They are receiving a much better education than I received. Their learning of math is built on a different foundation than mine was, and it shows. Those who think that neutrality in mathematics is possible need to think again. To be sure, some of these questions will not be raised explicitly when children are learning how to add or multiply. But this does not mean that certain answers to these questions are absent from the classroom.

We can return to history for some more examples of how subjects must be tied together with this integrating principle. The Declaration of Independence was signed in 1776. Surely *that* is a bald historical fact, whether or not the teacher is a Christian. Yes, but did that action by the colonists begin a revolution, or a war for independence? A revolution occurs when the government established by God is toppled, there are mobs in the streets, and lawful authority is rejected.[24] This did occur in the French Revolution, but not here. John Eidsmoe describes our war for independence this way:

> Many in Britain, including Edmund Burke, recognized the validity of the colonist's case. . . . At Independence Hall on July 4, 1776, they did not rebel against England; they simply declared that which was already an established fact—their independence.[25]

What role did the Christian faith play in this war? One Englishman recognized that role when he said, "Cousin America has run off with a Presbyterian parson." What relationship did the Great Awakening, and its greatest preacher, George Whitefield, have to the war for independence?[26] And was it a mere coincidence that all but one of George Washington's colonels at Yorktown were Presbyterian elders? The answer of course is that Christianity in America at that time was very influential (as a result of the Great Awakening a few years before), and the Christian church supplied great support during the war.

These examples from history and mathematics are representative. There is no subject where similar questions cannot be raised, and all educators must assume the truth of certain answers to these questions.[27] They may do so consciously or unconsciously, explicitly or implicitly, but they must do so. And when they do, they have taken a side. They cannot be neutral. The truths of each subject are related to God in some way, and that relationship is understood in the light of the teacher's worldview. But if the education is Christian, not only will each subject bear this relationship to the God of the Bible, each subject will also be firmly related to every other subject. Because the Christian worldview is based on the Scriptures, the students can be given a unified education. That unity is only possible because of the centrality of the Scriptures in the educational process. Without that centrality, true education will wither and die. With it, all subjects will be understood, and more importantly, they will be understood as parts of an integrated whole.

FIVE

THE STUDENT IN ADAM

THE FALLEN IMAGE

*E*ducation is not the downloading of information from one computer to another; the human mind is far more than an organic hard drive. Although education does involve the successful transfer of information from one person to another, the student is not a mere receptacle for knowledge. Biblical education goes far beyond transfer of information. To understand the nature of education, we must begin with the Biblical view of the nature of man.

How does the Christian view of man apply to education? We know that the race of Adam is in rebellion against God (Romans 3:9-20; Ephesians 2:1-3). All students in all schools were born into this rebellious race. Their allegiance to Adam continues until they are born by God's grace into another race descended from the second Adam, Christ (1 Corinthians 15:45-49). Any classroom may include descendants of both Adams. Jon and Melodie may be members of Christ, while Billy and Susan are not. Unbelieving students do what is wrong because it is their *nature* to do so (Galatians 5:19-21). They do wrong because they *want* to do so (1 Peter 4:3-4). When Jason torments some younger child on the playground, it may be because this is his idea of fun.

Nevertheless, each child still bears the *imago Dei*, the image of God. That image has been marred and defaced through sin[1] and must be restored in Christ, but it still remains. Although students are sinners, desperately in need of the grace of God, they have true dignity. J. C. Ryle addressed both aspects of man well when he said, "We can acknowledge that man has all the marks of a majestic temple about him—a temple in which God once dwelt, but a temple which is now in utter ruins—a temple in which a shattered window here, and a doorway there, and a column there, still give some faint idea of the magnificence of the original design, but a temple which from end to end has lost its glory and fallen from its high estate."[2]

This Christian perspective of man as a transgressor against the law of God does not destroy the concept of human dignity. Because man is fully responsible in his rebellion, he is treated as a *person*. His personhood and dignity are gifts to him from God and are to be respected.[3] In education, the teacher must maintain, at all times, this respect for the student. For example, humiliating discipline should not be applied in front of the other students. Name calling should not be done at all. The discipline is to be administered privately. The student belongs to a sinful, fallen race, but the teacher came from that same race, and they both bear the image of God.

The fallenness of people is a Biblical given, but should not be mistaken for absolute depravity.[4] Most people are not as bad as they could be, and neither are the students in an average classroom. While teachers understand that the students are sinners, they do not consider students a pack of devils.

Students are restrained from greater evil, not by their own nature, but by the common grace of God. By that grace, the image of God is not totally defaced and is to be respected. Francis Schaeffer made this point in opposition to the modern and mechanistic view of man. He said: "What has happened to man? We must see him as one who has torn himself away . . . from the infinite-personal God who created him . . . made in God's image man was made to be great, he was made to be beautiful, and he was made to be creative in life and art. But his rebellion has led him into making himself into nothing but a machine."[5] The point is that sinful humans are not machines; in spite of their sin, they have true dignity as a gift from God.

In his essay entitled "The Humanitarian Theory of Punishment," C. S. Lewis makes a similar point about human dignity, and he does so while maintaining a Biblical view of human potential for evil. He argues that to deal with criminals on a humanitarian basis, considering only whether punishment will mend the offender or deter others from crime rather than seeing it as the execution of justice, is to open the door to the greatest injustices imaginable.[6] In the Christian worldview, punishing someone for doing wrong is a way to respect that person's dignity. We do not regard the sin as a problem with the environment. According to G. K. Chesterton, "The determinist does not believe in appealing to the will, but he does believe in changing the environment. He must not say to the sinner, 'Go and sin no more,' because the sinner cannot help it. But he can put him in boiling oil; for boiling oil is an environment."[7] The wrongdoer must be addressed *as a person.*

The application to the education of children should be obvious. For example, if we constantly excuse wrongdoing or laziness in work, then we are no longer treating our pupils as having Biblical dignity.[8] In short, the Biblical view of human beings includes a high view of human dignity and a realistic view of human sinfulness. The Biblical view is maintained so long as the two are held in balance.

LITTLE HUMANS

How does the Bible's teaching on humanity's sinful condition apply when we come to the education of children? Children are not free from the inheritance of sin from our father Adam. In the Scripture, we do not find a contrast between innocent children on the one hand and sinful adults on the other. Rather, the contrast is between immature sin in the child and mature sin in the adult.[9] "Folly is bound up in the heart of a child, but the rod of discipline will drive it far from him" (Proverbs 22:15).

I have never seen a child who needed instruction on how to sin; it comes naturally. How many parents have had to teach their children to lie? Or how many fathers have had to teach their sons to lust?

On one occasion, I had to confront my five-year-old daughter Bekah over her bitterness toward her brother. Nathan, it seems, had clobbered her earlier in the day and had been duly disciplined. Her problem was plain and simple; she did not want to forgive him. I shared with her what Jesus said. "For if you forgive men when they sin against you, your heavenly Father will also forgive you. But if you do not forgive men their sins, your Father will not forgive your sins" (Matthew 6:14-15).

For some reason, she thought I was quoting Paul, and asked, "Who is this Paul guy anyway?" Now her questioning of the authority of Scripture was not due to playing with theological liberals or redaction critics.[10] Sin does not come to us from our environment; it comes from our father Adam. The links in the chain that bind us to Adam run directly through our childhood. As an old seventeenth-century Puritan primer put it: "In Adam's fall, We sinned all."[11]

The effects of the fall are clearly visible in young children, and a Christian educator must take them into account. If he does not, then all sorts of difficulties result.[12] What does education do when human sinfulness is overlooked? What do you get when you educate sinners? The answer is simple enough—clever sinners. Knowledge, by itself, does not make people better; it may make them worse (Romans 3:20; 5:20).[13]

Some of the most tragic stories in the Bible concern parental failure. 1 Kings 1:5-6 states that Adonijah had unduly exalted himself in aspiring to the throne. It says also that ". . . his father had never interfered with him by asking, 'Why do you behave as you do?'" David also failed as a father with Absalom, and his son lost his life. It was the same with Eli and his sons. They were evil, and Eli did not restrain them (1 Samuel 3:13). They too lost their lives. Samuel, who had been used by God to rebuke Eli for being a poor father, failed in the same area himself. His sons took bribes and perverted justice (1 Samuel 8:3).[14]

Such examples show us that just being *around* godly people is insufficient. There is no such thing as an automatic transfer of wisdom. The children of Christians have great privileges (1 Corinthians 7:14), but it is crucial that we understand the nature of those privileges.[15] To believe that children can be spiritually changed by their environment alone is behaviorism, not Christianity. Parents are held accountable by God for how their children turn out. For example, elders of Christian churches are *required* to have well-disciplined and believing children (1 Timothy 3:4-5; Titus 1:6).[16] But that responsibility cannot be exercised well if parents persist in acting as though education and environment *alone* were capable of transforming the sinful heart of a child.

Children, like the rest of us, are by nature objects of wrath (Ephesians 2:3). Those who discipline and teach them need to understand this fact, and they must recognize that how a child is brought up has eternal consequences (Proverbs 23:14). In addition, a child's upbringing has temporal consequences (Ephesians 6:1-4). That is, how a child is brought up affects his life here on earth. It is up to the parents to require the child's obedience, which in turn is blessed by God. This Biblical principle can be readily confirmed by a brief glance at the state of American schools and the future of their "inmates." As the first chapter stated, a grim future waits for many American young people. A major reason is that most of our schools have unbiblical assumptions concerning the nature of the student.

CUTENESS IS NOT GOODNESS

The first appearance of sin and self-centeredness in children often comes as a shock to Christian parents. The first time our oldest daughter told a lie, my wife was devastated. Despite our Biblical understanding of man's sinful nature, we still sometimes believe that sin is merely a learned behavior. When little Johnny comes up with some foul word at the dinner table, two things come immediately to mind. First, it is assumed that he doesn't know what it means and wouldn't ever want to say it if he did. Secondly, he must have picked it up from that Billy Jones down the street. Or at school. Somewhere else, *anywhere* else. It never occurs to us that Billy's parents may be complaining about our kid.

Although bad companions certainly reinforce the sin in the heart, they are not the cause of it. It comes from Adam. It is easy to misunderstand this because of the natural affection we parents feel for our children and because children are cute. Sin is cute in a one-year-old. He may yell and frown, and everyone still thinks him adorable. But we must remember that every moral monster our race has ever produced (and there have been many) was once a cute toddler. Hitler probably ran around the living room, delighting the adults with his antics. Our natural affection must be tempered with a sober, Biblical understanding of the evil of which we are capable. My father affectionately refers to infants as "little bundles of sin."

The Biblical view of man (and his offspring) must affect our view of education. Christians must distinguish the natural from the spiritual and stop making surface judgments. For example, children are naturally curious. This curiosity is God-given, but it is not the same thing as a love for learning. If a teacher is careful, the curiosity may develop into such a love. But if the teaching is poor, a love for learning will never develop. How many children have been taught to read only to grow up to a lifetime intellectual diet of the *National Enquirer*? If the child's natural curiosity is encouraged by a competent teacher, it will produce more than a superficial dabbling with knowledge. Children, like the ancient inhabitants of Athens, like to hear the latest thing (Acts 17:21). But they must be taught how to study a subject in depth and grow to rejoice in what they are learning.

One result of fallenness seen in children is the aversion to work, and natural curiosity is not sufficient to overcome that aversion.[17] Although work existed before the fall (Genesis 2:15), it became much more troublesome afterwards (Genesis 4:12). Anyone who has ever endeavored to get a child to clean his room understands that the disinclination to work is not limited to adults. This tendency toward laziness must be understood and checked. If laziness is tolerated in a school, whether in the teachers or students, then true education becomes impossible.

"One who is slack in his work is brother to one who destroys" (Proverbs 18:9). Not working is the same as destroying. In an educational institution, allowing students to avoid hard work (as they are prone to do) has destructive results indeed. We can see such destructive results all around us, and we have given it a name. *We call it the education crisis*. So for education to be successful, the student must be required to work. Because this requirement is not pleasant, the student must be motivated to work. But if the motivation is Biblical, it will not just be fear of negative consequences— there must be a balance between positive encouragement and discipline.

Those who state that laziness is one of the central problems in American education today are likely to be dismissed as harsh and insensitive. But if the work is not getting done, then *someone* is not doing it. The Japanese don't have thirty-six hour days; they do more than we do in twenty-four hours. Another way of saying this is that they work harder.[18]

THE PURPOSE OF TRUE LEARNING

How then are we to take the problem of the "nature of the student" into account as we educate? The best way is to address the purpose of true education from a Christian perspective. John Milton defined it: "The end then of learning is to repair the ruins of our first parents by regaining to know God aright and out of that knowledge to love Him, to imitate Him, to be like Him. . . . "[19]

A Christian education, in order to accomplish its purpose, must not see the fall of Adam as an incidental obstacle in the path of right learning. Rather, we are to see that godly education is made necessary by our sinfulness, and that the goal of this education is to "repair the ruins." This is not the same as saying that the repair will be accomplished by *our* efforts in education. God is the only one who can repair the ruins. As we educate our children, we must remember that unless the Lord builds the house, those who labor, labor *in vain* (Psalm 127:1). When Christian education is successful, it is only because God has given the increase (1 Corinthians 3:6). If He does not, then Christian schools will be every bit as barren as the most secular institution. We must keep our minds and prayers on the goal and continually remind ourselves that this goal cannot be accomplished by *us alone*. Then God may be pleased to use us as His instruments.[20]

So educational reformation must begin with the Biblical view of man. Without a Biblical perspective, we cannot know how to proceed, and we cannot understand the nature of our task. However, once the nature of man is understood, true progress becomes possible. With this as a foundation, we may turn to consider the limitations of the knowledge.

THE SOCRATIC SOLUTION

Many years ago, Socrates addressed the problem of the nature and origin of human evil.[21] If man is basically good, as Socrates believed, then why does he do evil? The solution, according to Socrates, was this: No man *knowingly* does evil. The cause of evil is ignorance, so the solution is education. Man can be saved from his evil through the educational process.[22] In essence, Socrates was saying that man can save himself.

The book of Ecclesiastes points out that there is nothing new under the sun and that what goes around comes around again.[23] Since the time of Socrates, humanists have approached the problem of man's evil-doing (which has obviously been a constant problem) in the same way.[24] Many today assume that education offers salvation; the humanistic approach to "repairing man" is evident throughout our education establishment.

This assumption was explicit when public education was first established; the promises made on behalf of public education were spectacular. Horace Mann believed the public schools capable of eliminating nine-tenths of the crimes in the penal code.[25] If only we established the common schools, our society could find a permanent resting place halfway between Utopia and the Big Rock Candy Mountain. Consider this assumption the next time some societal problem is reported on the evening news. Say a reporter has done some investigative work on some problem—it doesn't much matter what—anything from teen pregnancies to drug abuse. After the horrifying statistics have been cited and the heart-rending footage shown, there is a call for . . . what? Repentance? No, invariably the reporter will call for more education. We must have programs and more programs. We must educate our youth, our substance abusers, and anyone else who is causing any difficulties. If only our problem-causers are educated, then they will stop causing problems. The Socratic solution is still with us.[26]

Notice, however, that the approach is built on the assumption of innate human goodness. If we just tell people what they *should* do, then of course they *will* do it. Why would they do otherwise? As Socrates would say, no man knowingly does evil. This humanistic solution to the problem of evil reflects an immense amount of faith in man.[27] But according to Biblical faith, education cannot save. Education has set limitations. Christian education is no more capable of transforming men than is humanistic education. But true Christian education, grounded as it is in the Biblical understanding of man, comprehends the nature of the student (which we have already discussed) and takes it into account. The teacher does not interfere with the real solution to the child's problems, which is the grace of God. Christian education prepares the way for the grace of God, and it follows up the grace of God. *It does not replace it.*

Stephen Charnock, a Puritan writer of the seventeenth century, made this point with some force. In referring to both Jacob and Esau, he stated, "Education had not the power to root corruption out of either; no, nor out of any man in the world, without a higher principle."[28] So it is not enough to have a Christian curriculum, and Christian teachers. It is not enough for the school to meet in a church. The Biblical educator must not only have a Christian understanding of the material, he must have a Biblical understanding of the student. If he does not, then the result will be a hybrid Christian methodology employed to achieve a humanistic goal. The error is akin to thinking the Tower of Babel could have been a success if they had only employed born-again bricklayers. Man cannot be saved through education. It does not matter whether the knowledge presented is built upon false assumptions or upon true. If it is built upon false assumptions, then it certainly cannot save. But even if certain Biblical truths are acknowledged, that information *in itself* cannot save anyone.

What is the advantage, then, of Christian education? Why bother? We have already stated that Christian education must never be considered a substitute for grace. It cannot do the work of regeneration. Nevertheless, it has an important role. Properly understood, it is a preparation for those students who have not yet received the grace of God, and it is godly instruction for those who have. We must not make the mistake that Paul addresses in Romans—just because the law does not have a direct redemptive function does not mean it has no function at all (Romans 3:20, 31; 5:20). Just because education has no redeeming power does not mean it is incapable of being rightly related to that which *does* have redeeming power.

The teaching profession is not a priesthood. But if the teacher understands the proper role of true education, then there will be good results. I believe Logos School has a wonderful program and dedicated teachers. But we also have unregenerate children who do not appreciate the education they are receiving and perhaps never will. Fortunately, we have many godly students who do appreciate it. In Acts 14:1, we are told, "At Iconium Paul and Barnabas went as usual into the Jewish synagogue. There they *spoke* so effectively that a great number of Jews and Gentiles believed." This is what should be sought in Christian schools—not just teaching, but effective teaching. Christian content alone is insufficient. It must be presented in a certain way, and that way cannot be reduced to a *technique*. Nevertheless, God has graciously made it possible to bring people to the truth by *how* the truth is presented.

THE GRACE OF BESTOWED LOVELINESS

In *Surprised by Joy* C. S. Lewis describes how he came from atheism to the Christian faith. He was drawn by an inner hunger, and he chronicles how that hunger felt to him and how it worked on him for years. In the first chapter, he mentions reading a portion of a poem when a small boy.

> I heard a voice that cried,
> Balder the beautiful
> Is dead, is dead—

> I knew nothing about Balder; but instantly I was uplifted into huge regions of northern sky, I desired with almost sickening intensity something never to be described (except that it is cold, spacious, severe, pale, and remote) and then, as in the other examples, found myself at the very same moment already falling out of that desire and wishing I were back in it.[29]

Lewis had a gift for presenting truth in a compelling way. One of the reasons he is a master teacher is his love for his subject and his ability to communicate this love to his readers. Even if the student does not have a natural predisposition for the subject taught, the teacher's love for it will still be transferred to him. (It certainly was for me. I have come to love certain things simply because of Lewis's love for them.)

A sure mark of an effective classical education is a love for learning. If a child is taught well, he will not only learn the information, he will also come to love both the process of learning and the knowledge itself. Because knowledge is difficult to acquire, the teacher must require the students to work. But if that is all that is done, the teacher will only succeed in creating hatred of the subject along with competency to discuss it.

The history of Christianity is replete with examples. Otto Scott describes the education of James I by his tutor, the brilliant and orthodox George Buchanan. James Stuart received a rigorous and classical education, but it did not have the results hoped for. "Intellectually, it was the education of a Calvinist. . . . Another result was the creation of a prodigy. Still another, less obvious in its effects but poignant in its implications, was to place young James Stuart under a head tutor who hated the boy's mother."[30] The result of this educational fiasco was a cowardly homosexual king well-versed in the theology of the Reformation. The lesson should be obvious. Success in education cannot be measured by the imparting of knowledge alone.

How can teachers help students love learning? The Bible tells us that God loved His people while they were still sinners. There was nothing lovely about us which caused Him to love. Our love for Him is responsive to His gracious gift—we love because He first loved us (1 John 4:19). In the area of marriage, a husband is responsible for the loveliness of his wife, just as Christ is for the Church (Ephesians 5:25-26). When a husband loves his wife as Christ loves the Church, this love contributes to her loveliness. If he does well, her increasing loveliness will be seen by others.

What does this have to do with classical learning?[31] Learning is hard work. How then, can students be brought to love it? If a teacher is competent and a disciplinarian, he can make the students learn the material. But he cannot impart to them a love for the subject unless *he loves it himself*. True classical education is a presentation of knowledge adorned by the love of the instructor.

There are three types of bestowed loveliness. One is where an unlovely object is made lovely through an unconditional love. An example of this would be God's love for His people. The second is where someone who is lovely is made more so because of love. This happens when a husband loves his wife—she increases in loveliness. The third occurs when the love we have for something causes others to perceive or recognize the loveliness that is there. This is what happens when a teacher loves what he is teaching in the presence of students.

Whether or not the children acquire this sort of love is greatly influenced by the demeanor of the teacher. John Gregory, an educator of the last century, described a failing teacher this way: "Little or no effort is made to discover the tastes or experiences of the pupils, or to create a real interest in the subject. The teacher, himself feeling no great interest in his work, seeks to compel the attention which he is unable to attract, and awakens disgust instead of delight."[32] If the teaching is done poorly, it will hardly help to put more enthusiasm or energy into the performance. Again, Gregory: "The steady advance of veterans is more powerful than the mad rush of raw recruits."[33] Obtaining and keeping the delighted interest of students is a skill that must be developed and maintained through much hard work on the part of the teacher. Learning to transform that delighted interest of the students into a lifelong love of classical learning takes even more hard work. Nevertheless, if a school is to be effective in imparting a classical education, it must be done.

Education cannot occur unless information is transferred from one individual to another. Rigorous education results in a high level of information retained. But true classical learning takes place when students come to *love* what they retain. This can only happen if the teachers love their subjects.

THE HYPOCRISY OF ROUTINE

Sometimes an obvious hypocrisy crops up in Christian education. If the subject matter is in line with the Scriptures, but the attitudes of the teacher are not, a conflict is created in the mind of the student. What the inconsistent teacher writes on the blackboard and what he lives in the classroom are two different things. When hypocrisy is tolerated, it leads to greater problems. At best, the integrated Christian worldview becomes a dead orthodoxy—true words, but only words. At worst, anti-Christian living leads to anti-Christian teaching. Because the educator is in the business of transmitting a Christian worldview, he must also be in the business of living an exemplary Christian life.

But another type of hypocrisy is far less obvious. This is the hypocrisy of requiring students to learn what obviously bores the teacher. It is the hypocrisy born of routine. The student reasons to himself, "Why should I learn this? So I can be bored with it too?" Over the years our school board has interviewed many applicants who desired to teach at our school. When I have looked at the application forms, one of the sections of greatest interest to me is the place we ask the applicant to list eight books (secular or Christian) that he has read in the last year. Suppose, for example, we were interviewing a man who desired to teach history in our secondary program. One item of interest to the board would obviously be how much background he has had in history during his education—and how well he did. But the reading list tells us something less obvious.

Does the applicant love history *on his own time?* If he does not, then he cannot give to the students something he does not have himself.

One of our goals at Logos is to encourage every student to develop a love for learning and live up to his academic potential. This goal is impossible to realize unless the teachers have a real love for their subject. If the teacher is not excited about having this knowledge, then why should the student become excited about acquiring it? Necessity may induce the student to learn the material; it will not induce him to love it. If he does not love it, he will content himself with a lesser standard of achievement. The result is a travesty of education.

More experienced teachers must guard against the seduction of routine. Their lesson plans are all done, and they are not *required* to learn anything new—or so it appears—in order to get through each school year. This type of thinking is *destructive.* The students come to feel that learning is drudgery. A teacher excited about the subject will be extremely sensitive to bored students. But the teacher will also guard against the idea that students may be doing poorly because the material is so easy it bores them. At Logos, we do not consider poor performance an indication of giftedness. *If* the student is in fact gifted, the poor academic performance is a sign of laziness.

In an effort to reach students who seem bored, the teacher will set an example through his love for the subject. A good teacher will always be learning. But unlike continuing education in the public sector, the emphasis will be on the subject taught, not the methodology of teaching. For example, in most cases, a history teacher who does graduate work should do it in history, not in education.[34]

If the goal of imparting a love for learning is successfully reached, then the student will spend the rest of his life building on that foundation. Not only has he received the tools of learning, he has acquired the desire to use them.

PART THREE

AN APPROACH TO DISTINCTIVELY CLASSICAL EDUCATION

THE CLASSICAL MIND

DWARVES ON THE SHOULDERS OF GIANTS

Classical education cannot be defined merely as rigorous learning or even as a course of learning that enables a student to learn on his own. Requiring a student to work hard and equipping a student to learn on his own can be done in a vocational school; but, however necessary he is to modern living, a good TV repairman is not a classicist.

An essential part of the classical mind is awareness of, and gratitude for, the heritage of Western civilization. Russell Kirk, a well-known conservative and man of letters, states it this way: "Therefore we yield to the seers—the prophets and poets and philosophers of the Great Tradition—as authorities, because without their guidance we would wander hungry in a dark wood. The life of pygmies in the modern world would be poor, nasty, brutish, and short."[1] Kirk puts his case more strongly than I would in that he wants these men from the past as *authorities*; I cannot see how to get Heraclitus, Isaiah, Virgil, and Augustine singing off the same sheet of music.[2] But at the same time, Kirk is right to emphasize the debt we owe to them all. The obligation does not extend to a recognition of authority, but it does require attentiveness and humility in disagreement.

A classicist is not someone who agrees with *anyone* who has been dead two hundred years and whose books are still in print. But a classicist *is* a participant in what Mortimer Adler calls the "great conversation." We are not required to agree with them all, but we should know wherein we disagree. Ideological relativism is a *mod-*

ern development, and it does no honor to the great men of history
to impose this relativism on the past, as in, "I think we're all saying
the same thing really." Adler, founder of the Great Books movement,
put it this way: "Some basic truths are to be found in the great
books, but many more errors will also be found there, because a plu-
rality of errors is always to be found for every single truth."[3] This
attitude contrasts with that of the pseudo-classicist who feels that he
has entered this great conversation simply because he has obtained
a copy of *Bartlett's Familiar Quotations* and strings a bunch of them
together like wash on the line.[4] But it is not enough simply to cite
great names from the past, heedless of the great controversies (and
wars) they had with one another.

　　George Roche, president of Hillsdale College, sees this link
with the past as an essential part of education. "Education is precisely the preservation, refinement and transmission of values from
one generation to the next. Its tools include reason, tradition, moral
concern and introspection. . . . "[5] In other words, if we are not listening to the great minds of the past, we are not being *educated*.
Roche argues that true education comes to us out of the past and is
to be refined in the present. The modern mentality is that education
awaits us in the future, and we must go there and get it. Modernity
affirms with Henry Ford that "history is bunk." But if education
requires a conversation with the past, then history is foundational.

　　John Silber, the president of Boston University, makes a similar point when he says, "None of this is now a part of the common
experience—the common curriculum—of high school graduates.
This means that typical freshmen entering college lack the texts of
their potential humanity, even their spiritual survival. They will all
face, possibly before they graduate, surely before they are thirty or
forty, the loss of close friends or a family member, the loss of love,
disappointed hopes. Ignorant of these heroes of ancient Greece,
ignorant of Biblical heroes, ignorant of greatness, they will think
themselves historically alone, confronting a new condition unac-
companied."[6] When we compare the grief of David over the deaths
of Jonathan and Saul to that of Achilles over Patrocles, we do not
have to say they are alike in every respect; they obviously are not.
But unless we know of both, we cannot make the comparison, and
we cannot grow in our understanding of grief, both pagan and
godly.

　　There is an important humility in this. James Schall, a professor of political philosophy at Georgetown University, states it this
way: "On the other hand, there is no need to reinvent the wheel just
because we did not invent it ourselves. That is, it is perfectly all right

to learn something from others, from books. . . . We ought not to be overly surprised, then, if someone who lived two centuries before us, or ten, or twenty-five, can still teach us much."[7] The refusal to learn from the past is suicidal; it destroys the individualism it seeks to glorify. T. S. Eliot clearly identified the problem: "And there never was a time, I believe, when the reading public was so large, or so helplessly exposed to the influences of its own time. There never was a time, I believe, when those who read at all, read so many more books by living authors than books by dead authors; there never was a time so completely parochial, so shut off from the past. . . . Individualistic democracy has come to high tide: and it is more difficult today to be an individual than it ever was before."[8] When this chronological parochialism permeates education, the end products look as if they have been stamped out by a cookie cutter. Allan Bloom in *The Closing of the American Mind* argues that one of the things the American mind has been closed *to* is the voice of the past.[9]

In contrast, the truly educated student takes a broader view. Russell Kirk again, *contra mundum*: "And being educated, they will know that they do not know everything; and that there exist objects in life besides power and money and sensual gratification; they will take long views; they will look *backward to ancestors* and forward to posterity. For them, education will not terminate on commencement day."[10]

SHADOW AND SUBSTANCE

Conversation with the past is the heart and soul of a classical education. But it is important to guard against a mindless veneration of the past. The greater the tradition, the greater the temptation to exalt the trappings and neglect the reality. But folly remains folly even when it is learned at Harvard.

I recently and reluctantly saw *The Dead Poets Society*. My daughter had seen it with her friends, and the consensus seemed to be that it was a wonderful movie. I had my suspicions, but I thought I should see it to be able to discuss it with my daughter. The movie also came recommended by good conservative friends. The film is set in an exclusive boys' prep school where Mr. Keating (Robin Williams) is the new English instructor. In one scene, the boys are all taken down to look at photographs of deceased alumni. Mr. Keating points out to the boys that we are all worm grub and that they must—*carpe diem*—seize the day. But should Christians applaud an assault on absolutes simply because it is expressed in Latin in the hallway of a toney prep school? When Mr. Keating runs around like a dervish quoting Whitman in the class of a traditional school, the effect is comical. A school dropout, Whitman espoused a new kind of freedom based on the autonomy of man.[11]

Mr. Keating tells the boys to strive for excellence *because* there is nothing after death. Other more consistent applications of this kind of premise have been made by Dostoevsky and Nietzsche. The book of Ecclesiastes remains the best response to consistent nihilism. Solomon, without forsaking his wisdom, experimented with it and saw the void that exists "under the sun." He then returned to the fear of God and to obedience to His commands.

There is a difference between substance and ambiance; the former is the parent of the latter. When the substance of classicism is abandoned, as it has been in our educational system, the atmosphere produced by classicism is not *immediately* destroyed. This atmosphere can become a seedbed for the radicalism which so often runs riot in paneled hallways. But, as in the parable, the prodigal schools will eventually find themselves feeding the pigs, wishing they could have real food.

When I was talking with my daughter about the film, she said one of the reasons she liked it was the *atmosphere* of the school. It was rigorous, classical, traditional, and so forth. But the message of the film was an assault on all those qualities. This sort of deception is only possible because when the inheritance is being squandered, it remains an inheritance, and it still has spending power for good or ill. Prodigal sons are empowered to use their inheritance for their own destruction. Ancient schools, brick, ivy, and all, will not last forever. "When the foundations are being destroyed, what can the righteous do?" (Psalm 11:3). Answer: Start a new building on a new foundation somewhere else. It will take time to produce the atmosphere, but in the meantime it is important to remember what is important.

CLASSICAL CONTENT

In the establishment of our school, we began with the understanding that we needed to give our children a classical education which virtually *none of us* had received. This includes our teachers, administrators, and the author of this book. Nevertheless, this task is possible, although admittedly difficult, if we are taught by those who understand what true education is. We must go to teachers unaffected by the turbulence of modern education—teachers who have left behind a record of the nature of true education. We must resort first to the Bible and secondly to select old books.

This research will produce an education that is classical—because it is not buffeted by the latest wind of doctrine to blow out of our colleges of education. The process will be a slow one, but progress is possible. We can climb out of the hole we are in, but we cannot dig out. But there should be no attempt to be innovative simply for the sake of change. Lord Falkland stated it well: when it is not necessary to change, it is necessary not to change.

Because we are engaging in a *conversation* with the past, the first order of business is to learn the language. The relevance of such study is fairly easy for opponents to dispute; the target is as big as Western civilization, and it *does* move slowly. At Logos, we require our students to study the dead language *Latin*, of all things; and an immense burden of proof is therefore on us. For those content with facile objections, the case for classical study does not even require refutation.[12] While in other eras, the value of classical learning was assumed, today it is viewed at best as a hopeless anachronism. Is it really anachronistic? Should we return to such traditions for no other reason than that they are traditions? Didn't Jesus have something to say about mindless and slavish adherence to traditions (Mark 7:1-23)?

A SHORT LIST OF BENEFITS

The solid value of classical language study can be seen in five basic areas.[13] Various advocates of Latin study may emphasize their arguments differently, and their lists may vary slightly, but the following appear to me to be common ground.

1. The first is that it reveals a great deal about *English* and refines the student's powers of expression in his native language. About 80 percent of our English vocabulary comes to us from Latin and Greek. Students of Latin enlarge their vocabulary and enrich it through knowledge of synonyms that express finer shades of meaning. They learn underlying meanings of words, grow more familiar with the process of word formation, and gain greater insight into the structure of English grammar.

For example, at Logos we gave an English vocabulary test to some of our Latin students. The test involved English words with which the students would be generally unfamiliar. Some of the unfamiliar words had roots in the Latin.[14] The sixth graders who took the test correctly identified 81 percent of the words with a Latin origin, while they identified only 33 percent of those words not of Latin origin. Third graders taking the test did equally well. They correctly identified 85 percent of the words derived from Latin and only 33 percent of the other words. In short, the students were able to under-stand English words based on their study of Latin, and this without formal instruction on how to make the transition.

Similarly, the *Elementary School Journal* reported that in 1970-71 in Philadelphia, fourth through sixth graders received fifteen to twenty minutes of daily Latin instruction. The vocabulary subtest of the Iowa Test was used to compare scores of pupils who had studied Latin with scores of pupils who had not. And what was the result? The performance of Latin pupils was *one full year higher* than the performance of those who had not studied Latin.[15]

2. The second great benefit classical language study is that it enables the student to appreciate literature. By this, I do not mean solely the appreciation of ancient literature (for example, Virgil or Homer), although that is certainly a benefit. No, a student cannot fully appreciate *English* literature apart from exposure to the clas-sical world. Francis Kelsey, an educator in the early part of the twen-tieth century, put it this way: "No second-hand or guidebook knowledge can give the reader of English literature the feeling for reference and allusion which those of our writers had who were sat-urated with the classics, and which we must have if we would appre-ciate them fully."[16]

3. Another benefit is that it gives the student an understanding of the infancy of our civilization. Not only is our language rich in Greek and Latin words, but our culture exhibits a Graeco/Roman influence throughout. We see it in wedding rings, dollar signs, polit-ical structures, architecture, the names of constellations and planets, and of course, *et cetera*. If a student assumes that our culture plopped down from the heavens in 1776, then he will have very lit-tle understanding of it. Cicero said somewhere (who is Cicero?) that the person who did not know what had happened before he was born would remain perpetually a child. And is that not a central problem with our schools? They do not enable our children to grow up to maturity; rather, they perpetuate childishness.

4. A fourth benefit is that classical language study trains the student in the essentials of the scientific method—observation, com-parison, and generalization. The study of Latin grammar is a lab without expensive lab equipment. Latin grammar requires a great deal of *precision*, and the student learns to be precise. The result of this kind of language study is not limited to language; it carries over into other areas as well.

Dr. Fred Zappfe, former secretary of the Association of American Medical Colleges (1940), said, "In my opinion, Latin and Greek (especially) are the most valuable subjects in the college curriculum. . . . This association is opposed to too much science, and it definitely favors and recommends a cultural education, with the Classics as a basis. Personally, I would unhesitatingly accept as a medical student one who is long on the classics, especially Greek, and short on science. Physicians should be educated, not trained."[17] It has been fifty years since this was said, but the principle to which he appeals holds true regardless of increased scientific knowledge.

In 1911, Francis Kelsey reported on a conversation between a Professor Ramsey and the distinguished chemist Bauer. "I questioned him as to the relative capacities of students coming to his classes from the classical *Gymnasien* and the *Real-Schulen* respectively. I presumed that his best chemical students came to him from the *Real-Schulen*. 'Not at all,' he replied; 'all my best students come from the *Gymnasien*. The students from the *Real-Schulen* do best at first; but after three months work here, they are, as a rule, left behind by those coming from the *Gymnasien*.' 'How do you account for that?' I asked; 'I understand that students in the *Real-Schulen* are specially instructed in chemistry.' 'Yes,' he replied; 'but the students from the *Gymnasien* have the best trained minds. Give me a student who has been taught his Latin grammar, and I will answer for his chemistry.'"[18]

What is it about classical subject matter that has the capacity to train minds? Consider a small sampling of the demands placed upon a boy in the latter part of the seventeenth century in England. "In the fourth form the boys also tasted the delights of the Muses through a serious inquiry into the art of Ovid's *Metamorphoses*. The method of analysis was as follows: Each scholar had to memorize half a dozen verses, then construe the passage verbatim, parse it grammatically, list all the tropes and figures he could find, give the derivations of words, and show the extent of his Latin vocabulary by finding synonyms for them; after that he must scan each verse. So far, the pupil had performed only half of the usual assignment. Next, he must turn Ovid's passage into elegant English prose in order to turn it back into proper Latin, 'rightly placed according to the rules of rhetorical composition'; finally, he had to unscramble it again into a variety of English verse."[19] And why did that age produce so many intellectual giants? Gosh, I don't know.[20]

Consider the following thought experiment. Take an average graduate of a modern American high school, and take a student of the same age who came out of one of these seventeenth-century schools. Enroll them both at Behemoth U. in one of our remaining rigorous disciplines, say, chemistry. Who would do better? It would be a contest between a trained mind encountering unfamiliar material and an untrained mind encountering familiar material. The answer should be obvious.

5. And lastly, the study of Latin provides a great foundation from which to study other modern languages. The help it would be in the study of languages that are direct descendants of Latin is obvious. The student would have a head start on French, Spanish, Italian, and others (the student could have a good understanding of around 80 percent of the vocabulary of these languages). In addition, he or she would have a solid grasp of how an inflected language works, which would be a considerable help with Russian or German.

In short, the return to Latin is not the work of reactionaries. There is a solid educational value in it; the educational value can be, and has been, empirically shown. Those students fortunate enough to attend a school where it is taught enjoy an incalculable advantage.

SEVEN

THE TRIVIUM AND THE CHRISTIAN SCHOOL

I'D LIKE AN EDUCATION—TO GO

*I*n modern America, the fast-food mentality has penetrated the realm of the mind. The modern student has a mind full of McThoughts. Information comes to him processed and prepackaged, and he does his duty as a consumer. This does not mean that intellectual activity has disappeared, but having your mind full of mental "stuff" is not the same thing as thinking. This problem did not just arrive a few years ago; insightful people have seen it coming for some time now. In 1947, Dorothy Sayers, a clear-thinking classicist, lamented lack of true thought: ". . . do you sometimes have an uneasy suspicion that the product of modern educational methods is less good than he or she might be at disentangling fact from opinion and the proven from the plausible?"[1]

She goes on: ". . . although we often succeed in teaching our pupils 'subjects,' we fail lamentably on the whole in teaching them how to think. . . . They learn everything except the art of learning."[2] Her suggested solution to this problem was a return to an older educational method—the *Trivium* of the Middle Ages. This *Trivium* consisted of three parts: grammar, dialectic, and rhetoric. The three-part program prepared students for the *Quadrivium*—the study of various subjects. The *Trivium* equipped students with the tools of learning in order to undertake the discipline and specialization of the *Quadrivium*.

Sayers matches the three stages of the *Trivium* to three stages of child development. Grammar, which involves memorizing basic facts, goes nicely with what she calls the "Poll-parrot period." Younger children love to chant, recite, and memorize. Dialectic, the study of formal logic and argumentation, fits well with what she calls the "Pert" stage. Because children are argumentative at the junior high and early high school level anyway, they might as well be taught to argue properly. The third level, rhetoric, should accompany the child's "Poetic" phase.

When grammar, dialectic and rhetoric are taught at these ages, the teacher is teaching "with the grain." Two things are accomplished. The children enjoy what they do, and what they do equips them with the tools of learning. They are then ready for the *Quadrivium*, and beyond that, life. In contrast, modern educational method emphasizes the teaching of various subjects from the beginning. We begin with the *Quadrivium* and never leave it. This has the unfortunate effect of causing students to perceive each subject as a universe of its own with no relationship to other subjects. ". . . modern education concentrates on teaching subjects, leaving the method of thinking, arguing and expressing one's conclusions to be picked up by the scholar as he goes along. . . . "[3]

Although her arguments were cogent, Miss Sayers observed: "It is in the highest degree improbable that the reforms I propose will ever be carried into effect."[4] She was, happily, entirely wrong in this. She underestimated the power of ideas, or at least the power of this one. From its inception, Logos School has built its curriculum around the basic structure she suggests. Of course, some of our terminology is different, but our basic methodology follows this pattern. It is the purpose of this chapter to show how such a medieval method looks when dressed up in modern American clothing. We are happy to report that Dorothy Sayers was more than a competent essayist. Her thoughts on education have been put into practice, and *they work*. But the approach does not mean that our students have been equipped with truckloads of arcane knowledge of no use to anyone approaching the twenty-first century. Fundamentally, we are not teaching a different body of knowledge; we are approaching the knowledge we have differently.

GRAMMAR

We begin with children who have been taught the basic skills of reading, writing, and ciphering. This preparation occurs in the first and second grade as they are given basic verbal and mathematical literacy. The formal instruction in grammar, including Latin gram-

mar, begins in the third grade. This stage is concerned with the accumulation of facts since children of this age love to memorize. Our
students study Latin from third grade to sixth grade. In the first year
of Latin, we emphasize the memorization of words and the chanting of word endings. Dorothy Sayers made this point about such
memorization: "Latin should be begun as early as possible—at a
time when inflected speech seems no more astonishing than any
other phenomenon in an astonishing world; and when the chanting
of *'amo, amas, amat'* is as ritually agreeable to the feelings as the
chanting of 'eeny, meeny, miney, mo.'"[5]

Before I explain how this works in the classroom, it will be necessary to give a brief explanation of how Latin functions. In English,
we determine what function a word has in a sentence by its location
in the sentence. For example, "The boy sat on the chair" has a meaning entirely different from "The chair sat on the boy." This is true
even though all the *words* are exactly the same. In Latin, the function of the word is determined by its ending. Word order does not
affect the meaning of the sentence the same way it does in English.
So, for example, *"Deus mundum amat"* and *"Mundum Deus amat"*
mean the same thing—God loves the world. In order to change the
meaning of the sentence, we would change the *endings* of the two
nouns. *"Mundus Deum amat"* means the world loves God.
Consequently, the student of Latin not only must learn the various
endings for the verb forms, he must also learn the endings for the
nouns. Fortunately, as Dorothy Sayers realized, children love to
chant, and they can memorize by chanting.

This love of chanting is manifest again and again in our classrooms. When I taught Latin to our third graders, I could say, "Please
finish this—*o!*"

They, in unison, would then chant, *"s, t, mus, tis, nt! bo, bis,
bit, bimus, bitis, bunt! bam, bas, bat, bamus, batis, bant! ..."* They
keep going for a while; it is quite a spectacle. These are the verb endings for the present, future, and imperfect tenses.

With nouns, I could say, "Please repeat after me—*a, ae, ae,
am, a!*"

They would respond, *"a, ae, ae, am, a!"*
"ae, arum, is, as, is!"
"ae, arum, is, as, is!"

And so it goes. The children, of course, have very little idea
what this all means, but the memorized chants are very useful a couple of years later when they are in third and fourth year Latin.

They need to learn these endings because, for example, the
noun for girl is *puella*. Its different forms are *puella, puellae, puel-*

lae, puellam, puella, puellae, puellarum, puellis, puellas, and puellis. At this point, a skeptic might be tempted to say, "And so what? Why have the kids memorize a bunch of word endings in a dead language? Why not have them chant through some other collection of useless data?"

The objection can be met in two ways. The first answer is that in the study of language, Latin is not useless at all. It aids the student with his ordinary English vocabulary, and in addition, it can be a great help with technical vocabularies in medicine or science. As we discussed in the last chapter, there is great usefulness in classicism.

The second answer is that we do not teach grammar by teaching Latin. Each subject has its own grammar, which the children are at this stage committing to memory. For example, history has a grammar (dates, events, personalities), and so does geography (cities, rivers, states). So Latin does not supply the children with the grammar for, say, arithmetic, but it does lay the foundation for future language study. So we teach Latin grammar as one grammar among many.

DIALECTIC

In Gilbert and Sullivan's operetta *The Mikado*, the Lord High Executioner has a little list. If he gets his chance, the offenders on the list will all meet with their just reward. They include, alas, "children who are up in dates, and floor you with them flat." Mssrs. Gilbert and Sullivan were apparently acquainted with the "Pert" stage. This argumentative tendency is in full bloom around sixth and seventh grade. As children mature, they tend to use the information learned in the course of their studies in disputation. They love to try to catch their parents, the teacher, or their schoolmates in any kind of error. Instead of suppressing this tendency, teachers should use it.

> It will doubtless be objected that to encourage young persons at the Pert Age to browbeat, correct, and argue with their elders will render them perfectly intolerable. My answer is that children of that age are intolerable anyhow; and that their natural argumentativeness may just as well be canalised to good purpose as allowed to run away into the sands.[6]

This does not mean that educators give in to this kind of argumentativeness. Instead, the teacher molds it and shapes it. For example, in sixth, seventh and eighth grade Bible class, I have noticed that the sixth graders are by far the most questioning. "Why didn't God let Moses into the promised land? That was mean." "Why doesn't God make everyone a Christian?" Instead of squelching such questions, I have encouraged students to ask and dispute. If done correctly, this encouragement does not teach them that disputation is automatically good. If you encourage disagreement for disagreement's sake, then you will get disagreeable children. But if you teach them that it is good to question (provided the questioning is intellectually rigorous and honest), then you are *educating*.

We do not limit the encouragement of a questioning attitude to certain subjects. In seventh grade history, the students were studying the Civil War. Special guest speakers presented the causes of both the North and the South. The children were asked to do their own thinking and draw their own conclusions (supported by facts). The subjects the children study provide the raw material. The students are encouraged to take what is taught and think it through.

We noted earlier that the Christian teacher is not worldview neutral. But this does not make the disputation a sham. We want our children to have open minds in order that they may find and close on the truth. As discussed earlier, it is possible to believe in ultimate truth and pass that truth on to students without propagandizing them. One of the best ways to do this is to utilize the "pertness" of the average student. If they are going to question anyway, then teach them *how* to question. Teach them to recognize a fallacious argument, and they will not just hold the rest of the world to that standard; they will hold *you* to it.

RHETORIC

In the study of rhetoric, the student learns how to express what he thinks. The substance is settled; the question now concerns how best to present that substance. It is not enough to believe what is correct; the truth must be presented in a manner worthy of that truth. Obviously, rhetoric includes teaching speech, debate, essay-writing, etc. Style and clear-minded expression are important.

But rhetoric goes beyond the mere question of eloquence. William Blake put it this way: "Rhetoric completes the tools of learning. Dialectic zeros in on the logic of things, of particular systems of thought or subjects. Rhetoric takes the next grand step and brings all these subjects together into one whole."[7] Another way of saying this is that eloquence, properly understood, is not glibness of speech. The truly eloquent man grasps the larger picture.

The student who is being trained in eloquence should, therefore, be taught in two ways. The first way is obvious. It involves correcting split infinitives and the like. The second way is to encourage the student to draw from other subjects in his presentation. Breadth of knowledge is an important part of rhetorical skill, even though the subject being presented is fairly limited. It should be apparent that this is why rhetoric is built on a foundation of accumulated knowledge (grammar) and disputations about the reliability of that knowledge (dialectic).[8]

It is also important that this training in rhetoric not begin too early. John Milton objected to this mistake with regard to Latin and Greek; the objection applies just as well to English. He spoke of ". . . forcing the empty wits of children to compose themes, verses, and orations, which are the acts of ripest judgment. . . ."[9] Of course this does not mean that young children are not to begin the process of writing or expressing themselves in other ways. It simply means that such early attempts should not be treated as though they were the final product. Children should be praised for their efforts, but their efforts should be treated as merely a *step* toward mature self-expression. We should be pleased with what they do, but not satisfied.

Here is a table of the progressive learning of students:

Grades K-2   Children learn to read and cipher. Obviously, some elements of the grammar stage can be seen here.

Grades 3-5   Basic grammar is taught. The children learn dates, declensions, multiplication tables, places, etc.

Grades 6-8   The dialectic stage. The children continue to learn subjects, but they now challenge some of what they learn. This tendency should be drawn out and encouraged.

Grades 9-12   Rhetoric is taught at this level. The students learn how to present what they know and what they are learning.

Grades 11-12 The *Quadrivium* begins. The student begins to decide where he wants to specialize. This process continues through graduation, and on into university studies.

So then, rhetoric is the capstone of the *Trivium*. It is at this point that the educational process begins to bear real fruit. It is sad that because so many Christian parents have reacted to public schools, they are content with basic literacy. But this basic literacy can be accomplished in the first grade. This is not education; it is the first step. We cannot say that our job as educators is done until the children have been taught how to learn for themselves and how to express what they learn. When that has happened, the children, now young adults, have been equipped to face the world. Again, John Milton: "I call therefore a complete and generous education that which fits a man to perform justly, skilfully, and magnanimously all the offices, both private and public, of peace and war."[10] In short, they are prepared for life.

BASIC GOALS

From our inception, Logos School has operated under the motto "A classical and Christ-centered education." That motto stated in a general way the philosophy of the individuals who started the school. In 1984, the board of Logos School met together and committed to paper the primary objectives or goals of the school. It seemed good to organize these more specific statements around the structure provided by the motto. The list of goals was thus divided in two. The first section has three goals under the heading "Christ-centered," and the second section, labeled "Classical," also has three goals.

Christ-Centered

In all its levels, programs, and teaching, Logos School seeks to do the following things.

1. *Teach all subjects as parts of an integrated whole with the Scriptures at the center. (2 Timothy 3:16-17; Colossians 1:15-20)*

In order to be Christ-centered, Christian education must be more than a baptized secularism. It is not enough to take the curricula of the government schools, sprinkle it with prayer and a Bible class, and claim the result is somehow Christian. Secular education places man at the center of all things, while Christian education places the God/man at the center. There is no such thing as neutrality in education. Every fact, every truth, is understood in the light of a certain worldview. This means that history, art, music, mathematics, etc., must all be taught in the light of God's existence and His revelation of His Son Jesus Christ. Because the Scriptures occupy the crucial role in teaching us about this revelation, they must also occupy a central role in Christian education. In his critique of Christian schools, Gregg Harris notes that "inserting a Bible class into an otherwise secular curriculum does not a Christian school make. . . . The Christian school should be more than a good non-public school."[11]

This is quite right, and it is a point that needs to be made with regard to all forms of Christian education—whether in a private school or at home. Bible classes, Christian teachers, and prayer in school are all necessary for true Christian education. But many Christian educators, both at home and school, assume that such practices are sufficient to guarantee Christian education. They think that wherever these exist, Christian education exists. It does not. True Christian education requires that a Biblical worldview be successfully passed on to the students.

At Logos School, we hire Christian teachers. We are sponsored by a Christian church. We have many Christian textbooks. The children sing hymns and read the Bible. The teachers pray. But this does not insure the education will be Christian. When I walk into a classroom, I must view the students from a Christian perspective. Or, to use Harry Blamires' term, I must view the students "Christianly."

When I prepare a lesson, I must view the material in the same way. We have learned at Logos that true Christian education goes far beyond the mere possession of textbooks that refer to God. It is not enough to have Biblical window-dressing. It is our conviction that public education in America is failing, and that the failure can be traced to certain root assumptions about man and knowledge. In public education, those assumptions have been humanistic. It is therefore self-defeating for Christians to build schools based on the same assumptions. At best, such efforts will only return us to the public school system of fifty years ago. But it doesn't matter how many Christian flourishes are added if the foundation remains humanistic.

The foundational questions concern the nature of man and the nature of knowledge. Such questions cannot be answered without recourse to a certain worldview. The Christian answers these questions one way, and the answers affect the entire process of education. The humanist answers the questions another way, and the process is equally affected, although clearly in another direction.

2. Provide a clear model of the Biblical Christian life through our staff and board. (Matthew 22:37-40; Matthew 5:13-16)

When hypocrisy is tolerated, it leads to major problems. At best, the integrated Christian worldview becomes a dead orthodoxy; at worst, anti-Christian living leads to anti-Christian teaching. As Christian educators, we recognize that hypocrisy on our part will place a stumbling block in the path of the students. Because we are in the business of teaching a Christian worldview, we must also be in the business of living exemplary Christian lives. In a school of any size, it is necessary for the teachers to know that the discipline of Christian living is expected of them. And unless the administrators of the school are willing to encourage, admonish, rebuke, and correct, it will not happen.

3. *Encourage every child to begin and develop his relationship with God the Father through Jesus Christ. (Matthew 28:18-20; Matthew 19:13-15)*

Without regeneration, a Christian worldview and a Christian lifestyle are unachievable. If a man is dead, it is wasted effort to seek to revive him with a nourishing meal. If the life principle is absent from the student, no amount of instruction and example on the part of the teacher will make that student grow. We do have the responsibility to plant and water; we also have the responsibility to recognize that growth comes from God alone. God initiates growth in the life of the individual when he or she is born again. From that time on, nurturing instruction results in genuine growth as the Christian puts what he learns into practice. So it is not our role as educators to attempt to replace God's work in human lives. There is no way to perfect human beings by means of instruction, even if that instruction is Christian in content. The error of thinking that education can perfect man influenced the government schools at their inception and still governs their philosophy. To repeat this error—even with Christian instruction—will create a legalistic atmosphere in the school. In contrast, the good news that God offers us in Christ will create a moral atmosphere in the school.

Good instruction is conducive to rational Christian minds and godly Christian lives, but only if it presupposes and is built on the gospel. This gospel is: Christ died for sinners in accordance with the Scriptures, and He rose again on the third day. A person who responds to this message with repentance and belief will be saved. It is our goal to be used by God to bring every child who does not have a relationship with the Father into such a relationship through Christ. Then, and only then, will the rest of the education we offer be fully understandable. If the child already knows the Lord, it is our goal to encourage him or her to develop that relationship. As the child grows, the education received will further that growth.

CLASSICAL

As used here the word *classical* refers to the structure and form of the education we provide. It also refers to the content of the studies.

In all its levels, programs, and teaching, Logos School seeks to do the following things.

1. Emphasize grammar, logic, and rhetoric in all subjects.

The structure of our curriculum is traditional with a strong emphasis on "the basics." We understand the basics to be subjects such as mathematics, history, and language studies. Not only are these subjects covered, they are covered in a particular way. For example, in history class the students will not only read their text, they will read also from primary sources. Grammar, logic, and rhetoric will be emphasized in all subjects. By grammar, we mean the fundamental rules of each subject (again, we do not limit grammar to language studies), as well as basic data that exhibit those rules. In English, a singular noun does not take a plural verb. In logic, *A* does not equal *not A*. In history, time is linear not cyclic. Each subject has its own grammar, which we require the student to learn. This enables the student to learn the subject from the inside out.

The logic of each subject refers to the ordered relationship of that subject's particulars. What is the relationship between the Reformation and the colonization of America? What is the relationship between the subject and object of a sentence? As the students learn the underlying rules or principles of a subject (grammar) along with how the particulars of that subject relate to one another (logic), they are learning to think. They are not simply memorizing fragmented pieces of knowledge. The last emphasis is rhetoric. We want our students to be able to express clearly everything they learn. An essay in history must be written as clearly as if it were an English paper. An oral presentation in science should be as coherent as possible. It is not enough that the history or science is correct. It must also be expressed well.

2. Encourage every student to develop a love for learning and live up to his or her academic potential.

This goal is impossible to realize unless the teachers have a real love for the subject. If the teacher is not excited about having this knowledge, then why should the student be excited about acquiring it? Because our school has a good student/teacher ratio, the instructor has ample opportunities to encourage individual students. If this goal is successfully reached, then the student will spend the rest of his life building on the foundation laid during his time at Logos. Not only did the child receive the tools of learning, he or she acquired the desire to use them.

3. Provide an orderly atmosphere conducive to the attainment of the above goals.

There is only one way to maintain an orderly atmosphere in a school, and that is by means of strict, loving discipline. It is possible for discipline to be strict without ceasing to be fair or loving.

Indeed, when discipline lapses, fairness and love are usually the first casualties. There is no way to love or instruct a child in the midst of chaos. Our discipline policy includes the use of corporal punishment. This is not done in a way that usurps the authority of parents. When a child is being disciplined, the parents are involved at every step. It is our desire to be a service to parents, not a replacement for them. This attitude is true of the entire program at Logos, but it is particularly true of our discipline policy. We understand that many children who are discipline problems have deep-seated difficulties that cannot be solved by means of discipline at school. Nevertheless, our primary obligation is to the majority of students who require an orderly atmosphere in which to learn, so we do not tolerate the presence of a disruptive student. He must either submit to the standards of the school, or he will be subject to expulsion.

PARENTAL INVOLVEMENT

In addition to the emphasis on Scripture and classicism, we made another assumption in founding the school. Since its inception, we have been committed to the principle of parental authority over education. This commitment governed the composition of the first school board. For example, all our founding board members were parents of students at Logos School. But it took time to put this principle into practice in other areas. An example is the evolving structure of the Parent/Teacher Fellowship (PTF). As the school grew, one of the problems we faced was the regular low turnout at the school-wide PTF meetings. The meetings were hard to conduct because so few parents came, and if everyone had come they would have been impossible to conduct. Parents were very much involved, but the involvement was at the classroom level—*where their children were.* We had sparsely-attended formal PTF meetings and spontaneous, informal parental support groups for the teachers at the classroom level.

In the school year 1988/89, the structure of the PTF was changed in order to bring it more in line with Biblical principles. The basic reform was to eliminate the school-wide PTF and to replace it with a PTF for each classroom. This PTF is a small organization through which parents may contribute *directly* to their child's class and give direct help and support to the teacher. But we still have some school-wide PTF functions. Each classroom PTF elects a representative to sit on the school-wide PTF council. The council elects its own officers.[12]

What are the advantages of this system? We are aware that

most parents have their own child's interest as a top concern—which is as it should be. Most parents are not visionaries. This system makes it easy for them to get involved in their own child's education. But other parents have a broader vision or concern for the work of Logos School. They are enabled by this system to meet with other like-minded parents on the council. Our representative (or presbyterian) system also makes it possible for a concerned parent to be elected for a three-year term on the Logos school board. When this reform was proposed, the goal was to get parents involved in the education of their children. Because we believed the change to be Biblical and wise, we implemented it with anticipation. The results far exceeded our expectations. During the first year this system was in place, the amount of work done by parents in and for the school was unbelievable.

When institutions grow, the temptation comes to centralize authority and power. What has happened with public schools should surely provide a warning to private schools. All institutions are vulnerable to this temptation. As centralization occurs, bureaucracy grows. When problems develop (as they always will), people will sit around and wait for the experts (the appropriate bureaucrats) to do something. But if you want something accomplished, the Biblical pattern is to delegate responsibility *downward*. In short, the Biblical pattern of government is decentralized and representative. This is the advice Jethro gave to Moses when Moses was overly burdened by the work of governing Israel (Exodus 18:13-27). *Delegate!*

Any Christian school that sees the necessity for parental involvement must do something similar if the school wants the involvement to be more than mere tokenism. The PTF council represents the parents. The Logos school board does *not* control the PTF. The PTF can and does make policy recommendations to the board, as well as organize fund-raisers for various projects.

There are two advantages to this system. The first is pragmatic. *It works.* The second is that it provides a Biblical answer to the charge of parental abdication. When home schoolers charge that private schools can encourage parental abdication, the charge frequently stings because many private schools are guilty. It is not enough to say that you *want* parental input. Unless there is a structure to encourage it, it won't happen. For years our school wanted much more formal parental involvement. But until we reformed the structure, we didn't get it. It would be difficult to overemphasize this point. Private schools must have a structure in place that facilitates parental involvement. The structure I argue for here is decentralized and representative. A private school must honor parents with more than just good intentions.

NOTIFICATION

Another important means of involving parents is the communication between teacher and parents. Teachers must be very careful at this point. For example, many times the parents they have the most contact with are not the ones with problem children. If a parent is very involved in the class PTF and is active in helping out in the classroom, it is more likely that the child will be doing well. There is a direct correlation between parental interest in education and how the child performs.

But even with the best efforts of the school, some parents are nearly invisible. This invisibility frequently translates into academic problems for the child. When this occurs, the teacher cannot shrug and assume that the parents have left the responsibility with him. The responsibility for a child's performance is *always* the parents'. This means that there has to be a method of communication in place so that a teacher can keep parents informed, whether or not they appear to want it. Fortunately, most parents of children in a Christian school do want it.

A method used at Logos in our fifth grade class is the calendar system. The teacher has a copy of each month's calendar for each child. If the child behaves well, turns in all assignments, and passes all tests, the teacher places a stamp on that day. Each weekend, the child must take the calendar home for a parental signature. If a stamp is missing, a note from the teacher explains why. The system works. My wife and I and other parents know exactly what our children have been doing or not doing—on a weekly basis.

The school also has a policy of preventing unpleasant surprises at report card time. Because we have only four grades (A, B, C, and F), it is possible for a child to be doing average work in the middle of the semester (C), but to lose it at the end of the semester (F). Because of this, we have an F-day prior to the time report cards come out. If a teacher has reason to believe that a child is going to fail a course, then the parents are notified in time to do something about it.

These are just a few examples of the steps we take to maintain the position that parents are responsible before God for the education of children. There is *no* Biblical case to be made for *autonomous* private schools. Christian schools will only remain Biblical to the extent that they emphasize parental involvement and structure themselves in such a way to make that involvement likely.

WHERE THIS HAS BROUGHT US

Logos School opened its doors in September of 1981. Our goal was to provide high-quality Christian education for our children and to encourage other parents to take advantage of the education provided as well. The school began with eighteen students in rented facilities in the basement of a local church. We grew quickly—primarily through word-of-mouth advertising. The parents were pleased with the dedicated, loving staff members, the smaller class sizes, the consistently high level of academic instruction, the Christian environment, and the emphasis on classical study. As the school expanded in size and scope, bus service and a preschool were added. The math and reading programs were revised and upgraded to challenge the students individually.

By the 1987/1988 school year, about 65 percent of the school population scored in the highest range (75-99) on the annual SRA Achievement tests. In 1989/90, in some of our classes the average composite score on the SRA was 94 percent. The school average was 85 percent. This means that the *average* Logos student was in the top 15 percent of those who took the test nationwide. Remember also that this is in a school that is growing rapidly (enrollment rose to around 200 by 1990) and is taking in new students on a regular basis, which can tend to bring the scores down.

Because of the growth of the school, an intensive building search began in 1984. Finally in 1987 our board learned of the vacancy of a large roller skating rink. After negotiations, a special fund-raising dessert, and much prayer, the school was able to purchase the building with an adjoining acre for a playground. The school moved into its current facility after extensive remodeling in November of 1987. Additional improvements have been made since then, e.g., a computer lab and a library. As of this writing, we have been in this facility for almost three years and are already in need of more space. The Logos School board and administration are planning for further growth of the school, as Logos becomes a more integral part of the community and as more families become aware of the need for a Christian education and of the advantages of a classical education for their children.

EIGHT

THE OBSTACLES OF
MODERNITY

TELEVISION

C ritics have long pointed out that television is a fountainhead of
drivel, inanity, and superficiality. Since the invention of the box,
we have reared several generations of what I call vidiots—young
people mesmerized by the one-eyed brain sucker.[1]

Because of cable and the growth of the video industry, the last
few years have seen viewers becoming increasingly independent of
the three major networks. This independence does not seem to be
helping any. Some used to think that there was a vast, intelligent
viewing audience out there, uniformly disgusted with the cultural
wasteland of television. We now come to find out the networks were
only giving the folks what they wanted, and viewing independence
has simply enabled the average person to bury himself in the stuff.

Video stores have popped up everywhere, and the casual
observer who walks through will note that the shelves are not
exactly overflowing with "National Geographic" specials. Once I
was in a video store with my three children, and we noticed the family ahead of us turning in five or six videos and checking out more.
I am afraid that such families are not unusual. When do they eat?
Or sleep? More to the point, when do the kids do homework? When
do they read books?

Video dependence creates two major problems for the educator. The first has to do with the destruction of the rational and imaginative capacity, and the second has to do with the program content.

One time our family was seated around the dinner table, and I was giving the kids my "TV-rots-the-brain talk." The example I used was something like this: Suppose I said that Frodo was running down the hillside with a pack of orcs hot after him. How many pictures of this scene were there at the dinner table? The answer was five—because there were five minds imagining it five different ways. Now suppose further that we all saw the same scene in a movie. How many pictures of the incident are there now? Just one. The imagination of the filmmaker may be running riot, but the imagination of the viewers has been limited.

With regard to the rational capacity, all video, including educational video, presents "knowledge" in a severely limited and truncated way. Neil Postman, author of *Amusing Ourselves to Death*, lists three commandments for all video productions wishing for success, as they define it. The commandments apply equally to any attempts to educate by means of video. The first is: *Thou shalt have no prerequisites*. Every program, every video presentation must stand on its own. As Postman puts it, "There must not be even a hint that learning is hierarchical, that it is an edifice constructed on a foundation."[2] Postman argues that television is a "nongraded curriculum" and that in doing away with sequence and continuity in education, television is undermining the foundations of thought itself.

The second commandment is: *Thou shalt induce no perplexity*. "This means that there must be nothing that has to be remembered, studied, applied or, worst of all, endured."[3] Keeping the "student" with the program is paramount. If he switches to another channel, then all is lost. (Those parents who have children in schools that rely heavily on video for educational purposes ought to switch channels—to another school.) This takes us back to a point made earlier in this book that work for the student is, well . . . *work*.

And last, Postman presents the third commandment: *Thou shalt avoid exposition like the ten plagues visited upon Egypt*. "Arguments, hypotheses, discussions, reasons, refutations or any of the traditional instruments of reasoned discourse turn television into radio or, worse, third-rate printed matter."[4] As a consequence, education programs will always wind up in a theatrical context. "Thus, television-teaching always takes the form of story-telling, conducted through dynamic images and supported by music. This is as characteristic of 'Star Trek' as it is of 'Cosmos,' of 'Diff'rent Strokes' as of 'Sesame Street,' of commercials as of 'Nova.'"[5] But without exposition, is true education possible? There is a difference between being equipped to do well in Trivial Pursuit and being educated.

Postman concludes, "The name we may properly give to an education without prerequisites, perplexity and exposition is *entertainment*."[6] And there is no way to make a classical education entertaining throughout. There is work, pleasure, and joy in classical learning, but there is no slack-jawed staring at a box, demanding to be entertained.[7]

Of course, this does not mean that watching a movie destroys the imaginative capacity or the ability to reason. But watching hundreds of them, end to end, most certainly will. It is the difference between allowing children to enjoy a video and allowing them to become vidiots. Many Christians, aware of the problem of content (sex and violence), monitor what their children watch, and rightly so. But the problems caused by allowing the children to watch drivel will not be solved by allowing them to watch wholesome drivel. In this regard, the Disney channel and reruns of "The Waltons" are just as great a danger.

My wife Nancy commented on this problem in a guest column for our local paper: "In an age when parents are supposedly concerned about meeting the nutritional needs of their children (by avoiding that 'poison' sugar, among other things), it is interesting that they are simultaneously unconcerned about their children's intellectual diet. How many parents would allow their children to enjoy an exclusive diet of junk food? Yet parents allow television to fill their children's minds with intellectual cocoa-puffs."[8]

One standard we have found helpful for our home is a reading requirement. If the kids want to watch a movie, then they earn the right to do so by reading a certain number of approved books. I don't mind if my children enjoy a show; I would mind if too many shows resulted in an inability to enjoy and treasure good books.

The second problem concerns the didactic role of television. Children who are glued to the box may not be classical scholars, but they are students. They are learning all the time. What they learn may not be worth knowing (drivel), or it may be worth *not* knowing (immorality). In the latter case, the problem is easier to identify, but subtleties remain. For example, when it comes to judging the moral tone of a film, many parents check how much "skin" there was—or how many lewd jokes. But consider all the implied acts of sexual intercourse the average American child has seen, and then ask what percentage of the time the lovers were married—to each other. The answer is, rarely. What is the child being taught? Even when there is no "skin," the child is taught that marital sex is not normal (it is "unheard of") and that sex apart from marriage is the norm. He has seen for himself that it is common enough.[9]

What then, should be the response? If there is an apparent problem at school, parents and teachers should be prepared to discuss the child's viewing habits. This could take place in a regular parent/teacher conference or in a special meeting if necessary. If a child is struggling academically, the amount of time spent watching TV should certainly be examined. And if a child is speaking or behaving in an immoral fashion, then the content of TV viewing should be addressed.

Parents should distinguish between restricting TV as a punishment and restricting TV as a discipline. For example, many parents have seen a slump in their child's performance at school and have limited TV watching as a punishment. "If the grades come back up, the set can go back on." The problem with this policy is that it seems to affirm heavy TV-watching as a positive good, like food, air, or sunshine. When the punishment is over, the child goes back to a normal routine, which includes large amounts of TV watching. But if parents restrict how much TV may be watched as a *discipline*, the attitude is entirely different. The normal evening would include homework, reading good literature as a family, and so forth. In our family, we have read aloud C. S. Lewis's Narnia stories, his space trilogy, various books by P. G. Wodehouse, *The Lord of the Rings*, *The Book of the Dun Cow*, and many others. Reading aloud is a wonderful way for a family to spend time together.

Occasionally, as a break from the routine the family may watch something, but it should not be the norm. A standard our family has found helpful is no TV *at all* on school nights, with occasional use on the weekends. When families have this sort of standard in the home, the difference in classroom performance is marked. The reasons why are not difficult to understand. Whom would you rather teach—a junior high student who reads good literature for enjoyment, or a child who has seen each "Star Trek" episode three times?

MUSIC

The Closing of the American Mind by Allan Bloom caused something of a sensation when it was published in 1987. His criticism of modern music was not an incidental point. Rock music has indeed been *educationally* destructive. He writes: "My concern here is not with the moral effects of the music—whether it leads to sex, violence or drugs. The issue here is its effect on education, and I believe it ruins the imagination of young people and makes it very difficult for them to have a passionate relationship to the art and thought that are the substance of liberal education."[10] These are not the words of an old fogy, incapable of understanding a back beat. Professor Bloom has seen the connection between mind-dulling music and dull minds. He concludes: "But as long as they have the Walkman on, they cannot hear what the great tradition has to say. And, after its prolonged use, when they take it off, they find they are deaf."[11] It is possible that Bloom has overstated parts of his case, but the fact that he has a case is hard to dispute. Teenagers' extreme attachment to music is not difficult to see. In a public junior high school in our area, a student teacher was assaulted by a student. The teacher had made the mistake of trying to remove the student's stereo headphones after the student had refused to do so.

Apart from not allowing tape decks and radios at school, the Christian school is somewhat limited in what it can do. However, it can contribute through upholding high musical standards in band and choir. The temptation to slip into more popular music, even though it is often easier to perform, should be resisted.

There is much that parents can do, but that does not include prohibiting certain kinds of music without explanation. Blind legalism rarely accomplishes any of its stated goals. Excellence in music does exist. But if there is a musical void in the home, that void will be filled with something, and it will not represent that excellence. Parents should see to it that high musical standards are maintained in the home by means of the example they set. What kind of music do *they* listen to? As with video, the parents' concern should be twofold: Is it immoral? And is it musically bad? There is surely nothing morally objectionable about "Ba ba ba ba ba baran . . . ," but it is certainly not in the same league as "Immortal, invisible, God only wise . . ."

With music, as with many other things, Christians strain at gnats and swallow camels. They worry about backmasking, when it would be far more profitable to consider what is being said frontwards. They worry about a hypothetical demonic back beat when the song is just plain dumb. In short, parents should strive to set high musical standards in the home. If they do, their children will have another advantage in the classroom.

EMOTIONAL PROBLEMS

Children need to know they are loved. When a child is not loved, or when he is not aware that he is loved, serious emotional problems become apparent in the classroom and on the playground. My wife and I have an expression that describes the beginning of this process. From time to time, we have seen one of our children begin to act in an unusual attention-getting way. When this has happened, we say that the child's "tank is low," and we begin to pour on the affection. The problem disappears. But we try not to wait until we see a problem before we extend love. Our goal is to keep the "tank" full.

However, many children have been running on empty for years. In a school of any appreciable size, there will be a significant number of children in this category. They may react in one of two ways. One type of child looks for attention in the form of affection. He or she comes to the teacher for hugs, for example. Young girls frequently go to male staff members for affection. The second type of child operates on the assumption that any attention is better than no attention and misbehaves in order to be disciplined. At least when he is being disciplined, he is being noticed. This is not to say that all discipline problems fall into this category, but some do.

This is not a book on child-rearing. But how children are brought up has a major impact on the educational process. I was once talking with a principal of a public elementary school. He esti-mated that around half of his students came from "dysfunctional" homes. And while the Christian school cannot replace the parents, it must be available to the parents of children with such problems. In this way, Christian educators can be an encouragement and help to parents (servants, really), strengthening them in the task that only the parents can do. If there is a good working relationship with the parents, the teacher may recommend that they give more affection at home. If the problems caused by the child at school are major, the school should recommend pastoral counseling. It is a good idea to have several pastors sympathetic to school goals to whom such par-ents could be referred. Again, it is important to remember that the school cannot replace the parents, *and should not make the attempt.* At best, a loving environment at school will only lessen the problem. It cannot be solved there.

DISCIPLINE

In the area of discipline, private schools have several major advan-tages over the public schools. The first is that corporal punishment can be administered without the school showing up that evening on "World News Tonight with Peter Jennings." The second is that extreme discipline problems can be effectively dealt with through expulsion. This means that in a good private school there is no such thing as a permanent discipline problem.

Public schools have rejected these advantages freely and can hardly complain that private schools somehow have an intrinsic advantage. Spankings are rarely administered in public schools because corporal punishment has been wrongly identified with child abuse. But properly done, corporal punishment can be a very effective means to communicate love and forgiveness to the disciplined child. And public schools have passed up the option of expelling extreme discipline cases for ideological reasons. They believe everyone has a right to an education, and besides, *education* is considered the answer to all human problems. In the minds of humanists, to remove a problem student from the educational system is like kicking people out of hospitals because they are sick.

At Logos, certain offenses require a trip to the office. They are disrespect to a staff member, lying/cheating, rebellion or outright disobedience, fighting, obscenity or profanity. When a child goes to the office, he or she is disciplined (and sometimes spanked, depending on the offense). The parents are notified. If the child goes to the office again, the parents are notified again. The third time, the appropriate principal has a conference with the parents. If there is a fourth visit, the child is suspended. Expulsion follows a fifth visit to the office. Expulsions are never done lightly, but they are done. And through this means, the school assures that it can maintain a disciplined atmosphere.

THE PROBLEM OF MONEY

One of the reasons many Christian ministries are grossly underfunded is that for decades Christians have abdicated their social responsibilities. This vacuum, however, has been filled in most cases by the state. When the state assumes a responsibility, that responsibility is then funded through taxation. The Bible tells us to pay taxes to whom taxes are due, and revenue to whom revenue is due (Romans 13:6-7). This is true even if the taxes are unjust—it is possible the injustice may be God's chastisement. When Christians begin picking up their responsibilities again, there will be a transitional period where they will probably have to pay double. For example, I have to pay for a private education for my children, as well as pay property taxes for the maintenance of the public system.

There is a temptation to complain about unfairness. And from a worldly standpoint, it isn't fair. But it is God who governs the universe, not chance. I am paying double because this is what *He* wants. And why does He want it?

One of the things frustrating to the students I have taught in

Bible class is the fickleness of the Israelites in the Old Testament. "It seems like God just delivered them again from their enemies; they said 'Thanks a lot,' and a few pages later they are worshiping idols again. They get in trouble again, and then they have the gall to cry out to the Lord again!" What I have attempted to communicate to my class is this: When you turn a few pages in the Bible, you may be covering generations. What you read in your Bible only yesterday is fresh in your minds. But the Israelites may have forgotten the Lord's deliverance generations ago. Why? They didn't pay attention to history.

We are in the same position. Those who want to educate their children in a godly fashion today are doing so under a handicap— just as Gideon was threshing wheat under a handicap in the winepress. We are under this handicap because of our unfaithfulness to the Lord in previous generations. We surrendered our children to be educated by men and women who did not fear God, and we thought there would be no serious consequences. But there were.

When consequences become apparent, the appropriate response is *not* to grumble and complain. The situation should be received as chastisement from the Lord with gratitude. At the present time, the provision of a godly and rigorous education for our children will require major sacrifices. If the sacrifices are not to continue indefinitely, they have to be made with gratitude and humility. We have parents in our school who have a commitment that would be hard for many to understand. I think of Ann and Chris, two mothers who have driven bus in order to be able to send their children to school. They were up at the school first thing every morning, rain or snow. Why did they do this? Their children could have gone to the public school "free."

What are some of the sacrifices parents must make to provide a God-centered education?

1. Parents must pay tuition to a private school when they are paying for another school system through taxes. As the Lord gives opportunity, it is possible to gain some relief (by an override levy for the public school being voted down, for example). But there will not be permanent relief until Christians have built up a *mature* Christian school system throughout the country.

2. Parents must work in their church to establish sacrificial support of Christian education in the community. This support will take two forms. One, they should work for a church that recognizes the value of Christian education and teaches its members to act accordingly. I am talking here about a climate of support, not a legalistic requirement that children be kept out of public schools. In the first

place, legalism doesn't work. Teaching and encouragement does. For example, the church in which I am a teaching elder is overwhelmingly (and voluntarily) committed to Christian education. This commitment is reflected in the fact that only around 5 percent of the children attend public schools. The majority are at Logos, while some are schooled at home. Our church is in a university town where people come and go, so the percentage varies. Nevertheless, the support for Biblical education is overwhelming.

The second way a church should support Christian education is through finances. Is it part of the church's duty to support missions? Should we not support this critical mission on our doorstep? Again, our church has contributed heavily (and cheerfully) to Logos.

3. Parents, grandparents, and other concerned individuals should donate money to Christian schools. Christian schools, unlike most public schools, can be forced to close their doors. If they are put in this position, it will almost always be because of a lack of funds. The future of America is hopeful, provided Christians invest in that future. The best way to do that is to find a good Christian school and help it keep the bills paid.

4. Parents should donate time to Christian schools. In most schools, there are many jobs which can be done, and done well, through volunteer labor. The work could be maintenance, substitute teaching, office help, field trips, recess duty, addressing and mailing newsletters, and so forth. In many cases, when things like this are done by volunteers, there is genuine financial relief to the school.

TUITION TAX CREDITS

If Christians are financially pressed in this matter of education, then what should they make of the various proposals to provide relief? I am referring to vouchers and tuition tax credits. Such proposals can be good or terrible, depending on how the particular bill in question is drafted and how the Christian schools respond.

With a voucher system, the parents of school-age children receive a voucher which can be spent at the school of their choice, public or private. In contrast, tuition tax credits enable parents to deduct the cost of private school tuition from their income tax. It is clear that both proposals offer wonderful financial opportunities to private schools. But there is a major danger with both. What sort of school can receive this voucher? And what kind of school tuition will the government allow as a deduction? Public and private, yes, but it is quite possible that these benefits will only be extended to private *accredited* schools. An accredited private school may or may not be a high-quality school, but one thing is certain—it is a school on a leash. An accredited school is a controlled school.

If tuition tax credits become law, or if vouchers do, many Christian schools may seek accreditation for the sake of the funds. And then what if the standards of accreditation are changed? The school has become dependent on the money and cannot walk away as easily as it walked in. If schools are afraid of losing accreditation, what will they do if the standards require that the curriculum be state-approved? Or that the teachers be state-approved? Or that your drinking fountains be lowered six inches? In this sort of situation, the private schools have become nothing more than an auxiliary to the public schools. Christian educators who understand the battle do not want to be an auxiliary, but an *alternative*.

I am not saying that all accreditation standards are bad. Those standards that are good should be implemented in any school with high standards. But they should be met without sacrificing the school's independence. Meet the high standards, yes, but once the standards have been met, there is no reason to receive the state accreditation. Schools shouldn't, for the sake of money, give up what they worked so hard to achieve—educational independence. Private accreditation obviously does not pose the same kind of threat to a school's independence. If any proposed bill on tuition tax credits or vouchers *expressly states* that nonaccredited and nontraditional schools qualify, then it is worth considering. But if it does not, then someone should rap on the big wooden horse to see if it is hollow.

NINE

THE PROBLEM OF "PIOUS" IGNORANCE

IS IGNORANCE A VIRTUE?

*I*once had the opportunity to speak to a medical ethics class at the University of Idaho. Although the topic was abortion, afterwards a young woman in the class asked me about creation and evolution. Her real concern was over the relationship between Christianity and reason. A long conversation resulted. During our talk I discovered that she had been brought up in a Christian family, but her faith had been severely shaken while she studied science at the university. Part of the problem was that whenever she would try to get answers to her questions at church, people there would become defensive. I mentioned in the course of our conversation that there was no need for us to check in our brains at the church door. She said, "Yes, that is just how I feel." The tragedy was that the young woman had been made to feel that faith and reason were at war with each other. She felt she had to choose—she couldn't have both.

Here is an unfortunate example of the strong anti-intellectual sentiment that exists among some conservative Christians. There are two major reasons for this sentiment. The first is the result of mis-reading certain passages in Scripture, and the second concerns the history of the clash between the defenders and attackers of Christianity in this century.

Because of the nature of the education we are trying to impart at Logos School, the issue is very important. Is the attempt to pro-vide a rigorous, classical education under the auspices of a Christian school a compromise of the Christian faith?[1] Some Christians think so. I have been told before that Christian education should not be "elitist." The implication is that the attempt to provide a classical education necessarily leads to such elitism.

A MISUNDERSTANDING OF SCRIPTURE

In the book of Acts, Luke makes a delightfully ironic comment about the philosophers at Athens. Their futile speculations contrasted sharply with Paul's declaration of the gospel in that city. Luke says, "All the Athenians and the foreigners who lived there spent their time doing nothing but talking about and listening to the latest ideas" (Acts 17:21). The Apostle Paul certainly shared Luke's opinion. He clearly prohibited any sort of marriage alliance between Jerusalem and Athens.[2] He did not have a high view of autonomous human philosophy—nor did he respect eloquence as having great value in itself.

> For the message of the cross is foolishness to those who are perishing, but to us who are being saved it is the power of God. For it is written: "I will destroy the wisdom of the wise; the intelligence of the intelligent I will frustrate."
>
> Where is the wise man? Where is the scholar? Where is the philosopher of this age? Has not God made foolish the wisdom of the world? For since, in the wisdom of God, the world through its wisdom did not know him, God was pleased through the foolishness of what was preached to save those who believe. (1 Corinthians 1:18-21)

Paul goes on to point out that not many of the Corinthians had come from noble or influential families. This had been no hindrance to God, who chose the foolish things of the world to shame the wise. Paul also says, "When I came to you, brothers, I did not come with eloquence or superior wisdom as I proclaimed to you the testimony about God" (1 Corinthians 2:1). Paul was not a trained speaker in the classical tradition. He was not like Cicero or Demosthenes. It did not appear to bother him—rather, he gloried in it. His lack in these areas only served to highlight the greatness and sovereignty of God in salvation.

If this is the case, then why should we want our children to be trained in the classical tradition? When we seek to provide a classical and Christ-centered education, are we trying to mix whiskey and

ice cream? Doesn't Paul say clearly that a classical Christian education is oxymoronic? C. S. Lewis was very aware of this problem,
when he stated, "On the whole, the New Testament seemed, if not
hostile, yet unmistakably cold to culture. I think we can still believe
culture to be innocent after we have read the New Testament; I cannot see that we are encouraged to think it important."[3] He also
refers to the inadequacy of a pragmatic approach to this problem:
"I found the famous saying, attributed to Gregory, that our use of
secular culture was comparable to the action of the Israelites in
going down to the Philistines to have their knives sharpened. . . . On
the Gregorian view culture is a weapon, and a weapon is essentially
a thing we lay aside as soon as we safely can."[4]

But although Paul was not eloquent (in the classical sense), one
early teacher in the Christian church was.[5] "Now a certain Jew
named Apollos, born at Alexandria, an eloquent man and mighty in
the Scriptures, came to Ephesus" (Acts 18:24 NKJV). After his con-
version, Apollos employed his classical learning very effectively.
Luke says, "And when he desired to cross to Achaia, the brethren
wrote, exhorting the disciples to receive him; and when he arrived,
he greatly helped those who had believed through grace; for he vigorously refuted the Jews publicly, showing from the Scriptures that
Jesus is the Christ" (Acts 18:27-28 NKJV).

Paul himself appreciated the abilities of Apollos and encouraged him in the work he was doing (1 Corinthians 16:12; Titus
3:13). We see here that such abilities are not inherently wrong and
that Paul is quite willing to see them employed in the advancement
of the kingdom of God. At the same time, their absence is not an
insurmountable problem. The kingdom of God is not a matter of
words, but of power. So Paul is putting us on our guard against the
vanity of human speculation. He is not condemning those learned
men who have come and laid everything they have at the feet of
Christ. Every thought is to be made captive to Christ (2 Corinthians
10:3-5).[6] "I tell you this so that no one may deceive you by fine-
sounding arguments. . . . See to it that no one takes you captive
through hollow and deceptive philosophy, which depends on human
tradition and the basic principles of this world rather than on
Christ" (Colossians 2:4, 8).

If we look at this passage closely, we see that it instructs us to
be on our guard *philosophically*. The Bible does not require a philosophical know-nothingism. Defensiveness is not a good posture, and
Paul here requires us to have a good defense against the hollow
philosophies of the world. That defense is Christ and a proper
understanding of Him. It was C. S. Lewis again who made the point

that good philosophy needed to exist for no other reason than to answer bad philosophy.

At the same time, it is not sufficient to say that we should fight fire with fire. Lester De Koster, a former professor of speech, provides us with a good example of how a servant of God should balance classicism and Christianity. "Educated as he was, Calvin never lost his appreciation of the arts of rhetoric and eloquence; he preached sermons of enduring effect and could, when he wished, write powerful and eloquent prose. But St. Paul obliged Calvin to adopt the plain style, characterized by concise and simple language."[7]

A BITTER EXPERIENCE

When I was an undergraduate, my major was philosophy. I was approached at that time by a good friend who was a very sincere Christian. He thought I was not doing God's will in studying philosophy. He cited Psalm 101:3, which states, "I will set before my eyes no vile thing. . . ." As a student of philosophy, I spent much of my time reading worthless material—"vile" material. To his credit, my friend later changed his mind. Many other Christians, however, share his early sentiment.

One of the reasons devout Christians may be suspicious of intellectual pursuits is that long experience has taught them that the Academy is no friend. Many professing Christians have fallen from the faith through such study. My friend had reason to be concerned. It is much more likely that atheism will be encountered at a university than at a factory filled with blue-collar workers. The intelligence and scholarship to be found at such universities is frequently employed in the assault on Christian values and beliefs.[8] It is no small wonder that some Christians are suspicious about academia— and dubious about the Christians there.

Among various Christian ministries, those concerned with intellectual pursuits also face the temptation to appear "intellectually sophisticated" in the eyes of the world. If that temptation is not resisted, then a progression is inevitable—from faithful conservatism to "moderation and balance," from moderation to liberalism, and from liberalism to rank unbelief.

The loss of American mainstream denominations to liberalism at the turn of the century followed this pattern. Our major denominations did not fall into unbelief because they sent too many of their future pastors to Buffalo Breath Bible College. Rather, they went to the intellectually sophisticated universities of Europe, and they came back educated—and apostate. Consequently, American "fundamentalism" has been fighting a rear-guard action for most of this century. The posture has been reactionary and defensive. Once in this position, it is a simple thing to discover those passages of the Bible which make a virtue out of the current necessity. Once conservative Christians had been kicked out of the mainstream, many discovered the moral necessity of "separation." Defeat was thus baptized and presented as holiness.

Initially, this separation applied only to higher education. At that level, the unbelief was apparent, and Christians consequently retreated to build their own institutions. As time progressed, the unbelief of secular institutions became visible at the lower levels. True to form, Christians continued to retreat. Consequently, we now have many reactionary Christian schools that emphasize educational "basics," with prayer and a Bible class to fill out the Christian aspect. But because it is only a reaction, a full-orbed Christian worldview is still absent. The results, while educationally better on the "basics" than the public schools, are still far short of what should be done by thinking Christians.

PURITANISM AND KNOWLEDGE

Before the right kind of reform can take place, devout Christians will have to overcome their suspicion of intellectual rigor. If they look to the twentieth century for examples of scholars who are uncompromising in their scholarship and piety, the result will probably confirm their suspicions. But this does not mean that good examples are nonexistent. Probably the best example of balance between thorough scholarship and solid faith is given to us by the Puritans of England and America.[9] Piety and learning have gone together before, and there is no reason why they cannot again. It is worth remembering that we have much more powerful tools at our disposal now. One trembles to think what some of the more prolific Puritans would have done with a word processor.

The Puritans knew that all truth is God's truth.[10] Leland Ryken, professor of English at Wheaton College, refers to the fact that the Puritans were committed to God as "the ultimate source of all truth."[11] This led, among other things, to the study of science. One Puritan, John Cotton, said, "To study the nature and course and use of all God's works is a duty imposed by God upon all sorts of men."[12] When the Royal Society was born in England, Puritans were the midwives; seven out of the ten founders of that scientific society were Puritans.[13]

The Puritans were great advocates of formal education; in England during the Puritan ascendancy, the number of grammar schools doubled.[14] In America, the Puritans began to build schools just as soon as the basic necessities of life were taken care of.[15] The Puritans also had to defend themselves against the charge of "intellectualism," which is a good sign they were on the right track. Puritanism was not an intellectualized distortion of Biblical faith. The Puritans taught the way they did because they read their Bibles and sought to apply God's Word to God's world. Because they were human, the work they did was not infallible. The Puritans had their faults, but their general approach to education was not one of them. (And incidentally, neither were they at fault in their approach to sexual matters. The word *puritanical* is historical slander.) The Bible provides us with a framework to use in understanding all of life, and the Puritans took advantage of it. So should we.

THE FEAR OF THE LORD

Proverbs 1:7 instructs us: "The fear of the Lord is the beginning of knowledge, but fools despise wisdom and discipline." There is no better evidence of the loss of Christian *thinking* than the fact that this verse, and others like it, are applied to "spiritual things," safely detached from the rest of life. But consider the man described in 1 Kings 4:29-34 (NKJV): "And God gave Solomon wisdom and exceedingly great understanding, and largeness of heart like the sand on the seashore. Thus Solomon's wisdom excelled the wisdom of all the men of the East and all the wisdom of Egypt [*which would include astronomy*]. For he was wiser than all men—than Ethan the Ezrahite, and Heman, Chalcol, and Darda, the sons of Mahol; and his fame was in all the surrounding nations. He spoke three thousand proverbs [*including business and economics*], and his songs were one thousand and five [*the fine arts*]. Also he spoke of trees [*botany*], from the cedar tree of Lebanon even to the hyssop that springs out of the wall; he spoke also of animals [*zoology*], of birds [*ornithology*], of creeping things [*entomology*], and of fish [*ichthyology*]. And men of all nations, from all the kings of the earth who had heard of his wisdom, came to hear the wisdom of Solomon." In short, the fear of the Lord begins with a wisdom not limited to the Sunday school curriculum.[16]

Wisdom is not confined or imprisoned. Although many conservative Christians have withdrawn into an evangelical ghetto, the wisdom of God has not gone with them. Rather, wisdom stands at the gates of the city and cries out to the sons of men (Proverbs 8).

What she offers is more than spiritual insight about spiritual things; it is spiritual insight about *all* things. She speaks about political science (v. 15) and economics (vv. 18, 20-21). She knows all about the origin of the universe because she was there (vv. 22-31). All who hate her love death (v. 36). Those who build any school without her build on a poor foundation.

T E N

THE HOME SCHOOL
ALTERNATIVE

WHAT ABOUT HOME SCHOOLS?

*I*f the logic of parental responsibility is consistently applied, does it mean that Christian parents are obligated to instruct their children at home? How can it be argued that education is the responsibility of parents if we then turn around and delegate that responsibility to others? Whatever these teachers have going for them, one thing is certain—they are not (for the most part) the parents of the children. This sort of reasoning has considerable appeal; in the last few years, home schooling has grown at a phenomenal rate. In many ways, this is a truly heartening development. All over the country, parents have begun to assume *direct* responsibility for the education of their children. At the same time, the movement does generate questions. Is home schooling a Biblical requirement? Are there any possible pitfalls?

Home schooling is a clear alternative to the public school system, and in many situations, it is an alternative requiring a great deal of heroism. In the last few years, tens of thousands of parents have begun to teach their children at home.[1] These are parents who take their responsibilities very seriously. As one home schooler put it: "God is not going to ask the public school superintendent why my child turned out the way he did. He is going to ask me. It is my responsibility to see that my child learns about God and morality from me, and not from the public school system."[2]

When we first began the work of establishing a private

Christian school, the home school movement had not yet become the force it is now. But today, any discussion of Christian education that does not take the arguments for home schooling into account is necessarily deficient. The reasons for home schooling are many, with private educators and home schoolers agreeing on many things. As Kenneth Gangel, chairman of the department of Christian Education at Dallas Theological Seminary, put it, "Although Christian-school people and home school people do not see eye to eye on every issue they might discuss, their educational philosophies derive from a common fount—an unyielding commitment to Biblical education."[3]

Although on the same team, the differences between Christian school advocates and home schoolers can range from the trivial to the profound. If parents instruct their children at home for several years and then place them in a Christian school to continue their education, there is no fundamental difference in principle. But if a home schooling family maintains that children can be given a complete education in the *average* home (say, K-12), then frankly there is an important difference in educational philosophy.[4] The difference mostly concerns the importance of division of labor in a rigorous, comprehensive education.

A HOME SCHOOL CRITIQUE

Before an analysis of home schooling is offered, it is important to understand and respond to a home school critique of Christian schools. Home school advocate Gregg Harris lists five basic concerns about private Christian education. He begins by saying, ". . . many Christian schools only clean up the public school's practices. Objectionable material is ferreted out, Bible verses are memorized, and God is mentioned without fear of a lawsuit. But these are shallow, cosmetic tokens of what a thorough Christian education should be."[5]

The only appropriate response to this sort of criticism is a hearty "amen." Some Christian schools have merely baptized a secular curriculum. Such an approach should be vigorously rejected by *all* Christian educators. This book represents a partial attempt to do just that. But are there no home schoolers who do the same thing? Do all home schoolers have a comprehensive Christian worldview? Christian education (whether at home or school) should not be evaluated on the basis of those who do a poor job of providing it. A thoroughly Christian home school should not be compared to a half-baked Christian school, or vice versa.

Harris continues with his second concern, ". . . many Christian schools reveal double-mindedness. They want to give Christian children a Godly moral environment while they enroll non-Christian students in the interest of evangelism. The two ministry missions fight against each other and betray Christian parents."[6]

It is quite true that education and evangelism are not the same thing, and it is also true that a Christian school could lose its educational focus for the sake of evangelism (although I don't believe this is a common problem). At the same time it is important to point out that a godly environment is not one where sin is nonexistent, and all non-Christians are at least ten miles away. Rather it is one where sin is dealt with in a Biblical fashion. This is true both at home and at school.

It is curious that Christian schools are criticized by some for sheltering kids and by others for not sheltering them. Part of the reason for this criticism from different directions may be found in the fact that a good Christian school does shelter children from the presence of *undisciplined* sin, but does not and should not try to shelter them from the presence of sin.

At Logos, the overwhelming majority of our students come from solid Christian homes. It is true that some students don't have a Christian background, and it is also true that some of those with a Christian background fail to act in a manner consistent with their upbringing.

Those students who attempt to disrupt the godly and disciplined atmosphere of the school are dealt with in a firm and gracious manner. If they respond well, we are grateful that the discipline has done its intended work. If they do not, we are not willing to sacrifice the standards of the school in order to keep them enrolled. Consequently, the disruptive child is expelled. To use Harris's phrase, we are quite unwilling to "betray Christian parents."

Harris makes his third point this way, ". . . age-segregated peer pressure is part of the Christian school experience."[7] One of our goals at Logos has been to emphasize the importance of the older children setting a godly example for the younger ones. While the children are instructed in separate classrooms, the separation of different age groups is by no means watertight. In addition, the children in a Christian school have far more contact with older and younger children (on the playground, for example) than does the average home schooled child. This contact can be good or bad, depending on the disciplinary standards of the school, but it is false to say that children in a Christian school have minimal contact with children of different ages. Our own children have playmates who are both older and younger than they. Our children are full of stories about their time with these children. "Mom, do you know what Michael did on the bus today?" This contact is not occasional; it goes on all the time.

But Harris is not just concerned with "age segregation." His comment also points to the problem of peer pressure. What are parents to do when their children are caught up in the general excitement over Ninja turtles? If the peer pressure at a school is to immorality, then of course the disciplinary standards of the school should be applied. If the school cannot, or will not, apply them, then the parents should certainly remove their children. But if the pressure involves things that are not morally objectionable in themselves, then the parents have a wonderful opportunity to teach leadership and independence to their child. My wife and I have been able to teach our children not to allow the group to dictate what they like and don't like.

The fourth objection to Christian schools is this: ". . . too many Christian parents put their children in a private Christian school and then abdicate their responsibilities as the primary educators. This is clearly unbiblical."[8] Tragically, in some cases this is a charge that sticks. There are many parents who put their children in a Christian school and think they have therefore discharged their parental obligation. This was discussed earlier, and when it occurs, no defense should be made of it.

But home schooling does not eliminate the possibility of this sort of abdication. The Bible does not give the responsibility for education only to the mother. In Ephesians 6:4, we are told, "*Fathers*, do not exasperate your children; instead bring them up in the training and instruction of the Lord." In many home schools, the responsibility for lesson preparation, curriculum research, attendance at home school association meetings, and actual teaching falls on the mother. There is obviously no problem Biblically with the mother working with these things, so long as the father is truly exercising his responsibility as the head of the household. But in how many home schools is the father a passive onlooker? In how many situations has the father simply allowed the mother to run the program? If one were to attend a typical home school association meeting, how many *fathers* would he see there?

Abdication is a problem in Christian schools *and* home schools. It need not be a problem in *either*. For many of our families at Logos, there is no abdication at all. The parents are actively involved in the education of their children. For example, many of the Logos parents are at the school virtually every day. They go on field trips, drive the bus, help in the office, work in the classrooms and the library, come into the classes as guest speakers, and so forth. My wife has been a teacher, newsletter proofreader, volunteer teacher, substitute teacher, teacher's aide, not to mention much work done behind the scenes.[9] In a good Christian school, a committed parent should be able to be as involved as he or she wants to be.

The last concern Harris raises has to do with classroom organization. "Fifth, Christian schools that use classroom organization inevitably face the problem of dividing the teacher's time among a class full of students, all of whom have differing needs." This is a very real problem, as anyone who has ever taught in a classroom would testify. Some children learn a concept right away, and others take their sweet time. But again, how is this problem limited to a classroom? A teacher who has twenty eight-year-olds and a basic lesson in math will be confronted with a moderate range of abilities. (If the range is extreme, a child could be advanced or set behind a grade.) But the moderate range of abilities does present the teacher with a problem.

Harris described this problem as one of "dividing the teacher's time." But what about a home school mom who is teaching a twelve-year-old, a ten-year-old, and an eight-year-old, and she has to teach each one of them history, math, English, science, etc.? Is she not faced with a problem in "dividing her time"? And may not an overwhelmed home schooler be tempted to avoid a difficult or disliked subject?

The best way to divide time efficiently is through a division of labor. Good home schoolers do take advantage of the division of labor. But there are built-in limits to their ability to do so and remain a home school. If they bring in outsiders to help, at some point the use of these people will turn the endeavor into something beyond a home school.

I believe that a Christian school provides Christian parents with the most efficient way to take responsibility for the education of their children, while at the same time ensuring that true education actually happens. In other words, because there is division of labor a thorough education can be provided. Because the division of labor is between Christians who know one another well, parents do not have to choose between parental responsibility and rigorous academics.

BURNOUT

Raymond and Dorothy Moore, who were instrumental in getting the home school movement off the ground, have recently written a book entitled *Home School Burnout*. The fact that it was necessary to write such a book indicates one of the fundamental problems with home schooling. Some parents who try to compete with schools become frustrated and unsuccessful. Their choice is burnout on the one hand and changing the structure of the home school on the other. But it should be obvious that changing the structure of the schooling received by the child will change the nature of the education itself. Unfortunately, changing the structure can actually result in a lowering of academic standards.

It is not difficult then for some home school parents to make a virtue out of necessity and abandon the traditional pattern of child instruction. This is one of the more disturbing developments in the theory of home schooling. As the Moores argue, "They (the children) would have been far better off *wherever possible* waiting until ages eight to ten or later to start formal studies (at home or school) in the second, third, fourth or fifth grade. They would then quickly pass early entrants in learning, behavior and sociability."[10] One friend of mine, a home schooler, is really concerned about this emphasis. He and his wife started the education of their children early, and have done a remarkable job. But he knows of someone else in the home schooling movement, in trouble with the education establishment, who believes she can wait until her children are twelve to teach them to read. In my friend's words, the woman is "making her own trouble."[11]

Another problem with home schooling is a common, but mistaken, assumption about human nature. We have already covered the Biblical view of man and how it should affect the process of education. (Chapter 4—the sin of laziness comes from Adam, not the public schools.) But there seems to be a prejudice among some home schoolers against "forced learning," and the prejudice appears to be based on an overly optimistic view of the child's innate love of learning. For example, one advocate of home schools writes, "Deep within, your children already naturally, organically love to learn. Let them *intrinsically*—inside themselves—feel the joy and excitement, because therein lay (*sic*) the true, natural, most highly motivating reward—and the most highly effective learning. Once you and they are able to rekindle that joy they were born with, motivation and learning for them will never cease."[12] I am afraid that there is more than a little sentimentalism here, with the nature and power of sin being overlooked. Many children need to be disciplined in an intellectual way *early*. If they are not, then the opportunity is lost; a mental laziness is already habitual.

The alternative is for the home school parents to keep pace generally with the curricula of the more traditional Christian school.

Some parents are quite capable of doing this; many are not. As a rule, the average parent who attempts to keep pace with the education that goes on in a *good* school will have increasing difficulty as the years go by. Many parents can do an outstanding job the first several years. But it is one thing to teach your five-year old how to read and quite another to teach Latin to an eleven-year-old. For starters, you have to know Latin to teach it. At a Christian school, if one teacher knows Latin, then twenty students can learn it. But in order for twenty students in home schools to learn Latin, twenty teachers have to learn it. This is an *inefficient* division of labor, which leads to burnout.

If home schoolers attempt to solve this problem by having all the children among the various families learn from just one teacher, then we have the rudiments of a new alternative Christian school.[13] This same problem applies to any field of specialized knowledge not common to all parents—music, foreign languages, advanced science, advanced math, etc. The reason home schooling works so well at the early years is that the parents are teaching literacy, and they are all literate. *This is not true of subjects later in the curriculum.*

Of course, there are many curricula designed for home schoolers which take this lack of educational background on the part of the parent into account. But why is it legitimate for parents to delegate the responsibility for *research* to others, but not legitimate to delegate the responsibility for actual teaching? Suppose a Christian parent tells his child that Napoleon did thus and such, on the strength of the research done by Smith down at XYZ Textbooks? Shouldn't the parent do his own research? The answer to this, of course, is that the responsibility of parents is not to do everything themselves. The Scriptures require parents to provide food for their children; it does not require every father to be a farmer, growing the food his children will eat. The key is responsible, diligent oversight.[14]

So the best form of home schooling is that which takes some advantage of a division of labor. For example, the research that Mary Pride did for the *Big Book of Home Learning* is research that other parents won't have to do.[15] Home schooling of this sort is what our family would do if a solid Christian school were not available.[16] At the same time, I believe the best way to oversee the education of our children is to find or start a Christian school that encourages parental involvement.

In a good Christian school, the parents know their children's teachers very well. They should know *what* the children are being taught and *how* they are being taught. In short, they are responsible before God to monitor everything that is going into the child's mind. If a Christian school is a *Biblical* school, it will strongly encourage such parental involvement.[17] The fact is, a parent can have a personal relationship with his child's teachers, each of whom has a specialized field of knowledge. This provides the parent with a more effective means of oversight than is possible when information is received through the mail.

CONCLUSION

I am concerned that this chapter not be perceived as too "adversarial." My wife and I would certainly home school our children if a good Christian school were not available. Fortunately, we have one. Compared to public education, home schooling generally has much to commend it. According to one study, home schooled children performed quite well on standardized achievement tests; in a doctoral dissertation on home schooling, Alberta Griffiths reported on a study of 426 home schoolers in the state of Washington. The study "concluded that the students scored as well or better than their peers across the nation on virtually all of the six test scales measured by the Stanford Achievement Test."[18]

But remember that this is a comparison between home schools and American public schools, which are a global embarrassment. So when I say we would home school, it is important to remember the difficulty of the task. It is important to count the cost and not leave unfinished endeavors behind us. At this writing, my wife teaches three of the secondary English classes at Logos, and I have taught Latin, logic, Bible, civics, and debate. We are both college-educated and extremely committed to Christian education. Nevertheless, if we had to continue our children's education *at the same level that Logos provides*, we would be extremely pressed. In just a few more years, it would become impossible to maintain the same standards. Just thinking about high school chemistry makes this student of the humanities shudder. So part of the reason home schoolers are capable of outperforming the public schools has to do with the horrible condition of the schools. I feel confident that my wife and I could compete in this same way. But if we had to compete with a school that was functioning as a school *should*, I am not nearly as optimistic.

PART FOUR

CONCLUSIONS

ELEVEN

THE LIMITS OF THE STATE: A SUMMARY

THE STATE AND THE ART

*A*s we have seen already, many champions of the public school system are fully aware of its defects. There is no shortage of proposed reforms, many of them brilliant and to the point. Are these reforms likely to be implemented? *Can* they be?

For the first time in many generations, the American educational system is producing a generation of children less educated than their parents.[1] It is a frightening thought; more frightening, however, is the possibility that not much can be done about it. The more the fruit of educational folly becomes apparent, the more we hear calls for better-funded educational folly. And will we continue to hear suggestions, criticisms, and jeremiads from frustrated reformers? You bet.

Why is this? Many of the critics and reformers of the public schools have begun their analysis with a mistaken assumption. Because the failure of our educational system *to educate* has been so obvious, they have made the mistake of assuming the education establishment is failing. They also assumed the goal of this establishment is the education of children. But the *definition* of education varies according to the worldview of the educator—and besides, education bureaucracies, like all bureaucracies, tend to replace their original task with the goal of self-perpetuation. And in the achievement of *that* goal there has been tremendous success.

If home schools produced an illiteracy rate that even came

close to the one generated by the public schools, they would be shut down. If private schools tried to graduate students who couldn't read, the local educational authorities would be all over them. Why? Because education is supposed to educate. But if state schools fail at their task, it is because more funding is urgently needed. Why? Because the public education establishment wants to perpetuate the public education establishment, and *anything* can be used as an argument to that end.

Consider this testimony before the Labor and Human Resources Committee of the U. S. Senate. Mary Hatwood Futrell, president of the NEA, was presenting the position of NEA on a proposed National Board for Professional Teaching Standards. She said, "Given that autonomy is an essential element of the Board, federal assistance for this initial research function of the Board must be free of encumbrances or preconceptions about what the results of that research would be."[2] In other words, the federal assistance would not be declined, but any expectations about results were out of order. The establishment is failing, and so the role of the establishment must be enlarged with no accountability. Her testimony also made clear the fact that the NEA would demand that the Board be a part of the public education establishment; the NEA wanted the Board to be comprised of a majority of practicing public school teachers.[3]

If private educators don't educate, they have to face the consequences, which fall on the school or home. If public educators do not educate, the negative consequences fall on the students who are not properly equipped to face life. The worldview the public schools represent looks to institutional solutions and saviors in any crisis. Consequently, with the growth of problems (no matter who caused them), it is easy to call for more support for our educational institutions. They now have another crisis (i.e., an unaccountable rampaging epidemic of dyslexia), which requires more funding or programs to solve.

This is the basic question: what mechanism exists (or could exist) that would be able to bring about genuine reform in the state schools? There is only one pressure strong enough—the possibility of a loss of funding, and the only thing powerful enough to accomplish *that* is a free market in education. But this is like saying that the problem with a government program is, well, the fact that it is a government program. Public schools, by definition, are not private. Can they be reformed and remain state-controlled? There are strong arguments which say no. The overwhelming state control insulates the schools from market forces and makes them the pawn of special interest groups (the NEA is the obvious example).

It is not my purpose here to provide a critique of intrusive government and a defense of free markets. That has been effectively done elsewhere.[4] For our purpose we may consider it an established economic fact that when a government runs or controls a widget factory, it is not long before there is a shortage of widgets. Now the objective of those running the widget factory remains the same as before (staying in business). But in a free market, the means to the objective had been to make and sell as many widgets as possible, and this depends upon the satisfaction of those receiving the product. After the government gets into the act, the objective cannot be achieved through market performance. But it *can* be achieved through political pressure.

The various critiques of intrusive government have demonstrated that inefficiency, corruption, product shortages, and so forth are all endemic to this approach. They are not corruptions of the approach, they are *manifestations* of it. So the question really is why so few have applied the arguments against government-controlled widgets to government-controlled education. It is surprising that many conservatives fail to see the implications. There is a connection between the failure of education and the fact that it is a service provided by government, apart from market forces. When a service is provided outside the market, what, of necessity, happens to the service?

Those who want to reform the system through various structural and curricular means have overlooked the most obvious structural feature of public education—the fact that it is *public*. There is no *physical* reason why the Post Office can't get a package across the country as fast as UPS, but there is still a reason. In the same way, there is no physical reason these reforms couldn't be implemented in the public school system, but it is not going to happen.

The reforms listed earlier in this book will not be voluntarily instituted. There is no *reason* to. Beyond this, there is reason not to. Bureaucracies will always maintain the status quo—even when the status quo is a disaster. This is especially the case when the reforms bring some form of market pressure or competition to the public school. In the market, private schools are in their natural habitat. Public schools, when they compete at all, will do so poorly. Most of the time public schools will defend their position through political means.

A good example of refusal to compete in the market has been the response of the education establishment to phonics instruction in private education. The public schools simply will not abandon the "look/say" method of teaching reading.[6] If all public schools adopted strict phonics instruction,[7] what would happen? The schools would lose funding for many of the special programs designed to help the casualties of the "look/say" method. So why should they adopt phonics instruction? It may help the students, but it hurts the programs. A cynic might say that their problem is simply one of greed; petty bureaucrats tend to sandbag themselves in their positions of financial security, whether or not the mission is being accomplished. But it would be closer to the mark to recognize the collision of faiths here; the problem is one of conflicting world-views. To abandon the institutional solutions is to acknowledge that the worldview is flawed. Our education crisis is at bottom a crisis of faith. It is long overdue.

Logos School operates in the market. We have *customers*. It is important for us to keep our customers pleased with the job we are doing. Put in Biblical terms, we are their servants. This means that when we hear of some means to improve our work, we have a reason to take advantage of it immediately. In a public school, it is not necessary to please the customers, the parents. In fact, over time, the education establishment forgets that they are customers. However, the pressure *is* on to please the teachers because of fear of strikes, etc. In this political world, the pressure is to please the education lobby.

POOR MOTIVATION FOR POOR TEACHERS

The lack of market forces in public education does not just affect the schools. It also affects potential teachers. When the motivation of pleasing the customer is removed, other motivations arise. Government control does not affect *whether* people will be motivated to undertake the job, but rather *how* they will be motivated.

Broadly speaking, basic motivations for entering the teaching profession today may be reduced to two—ideological and personal. The ideological educator is a social engineer. He or she wants to mold and shape future generations according to some template in the mind. The behavior of some educators during the nuclear freeze movement a few years back is a good example. (*"Dear editor, Why do people want to blow up the world? I don't want to get hurt. Please stop making bombs. Suzy Jones, age 6."*)[8] Following John Dewey, one of the fathers of the modern public schools, these educators are interested in education as a tool for reshaping society. The pattern they have in mind would be vigorously opposed by many parents—provided the parents knew the real agenda.[9]

Personal reasons vary. Some teachers are born educators and have a deep love for children. They couldn't be happy doing anything else. Or the teacher may have a real excitement and love for the subject. Teachers with this motivation are valuable indeed, but they are frequently discouraged and frustrated in the public schools. The structure of the system is against them. There are other personal reasons not so admirable. Say a college student has a low grade point average, wants reasonable pay, and an indoor job with no heavy lifting. As Murray points out, "Overall, teachers are drawn not just from the average college graduates, which would itself be cause for concern, but from the below average."[10] For such individuals, the current educational system is ideal.

A prevailing belief within education colleges holds that teachers need to be taught the methodology of teaching instead of mastering the subject matter they will teach. Thus, someone with a degree in education may teach mathematics, English, history, and the like. Someone with a degree in mathematics could not teach mathematics. Someone with a degree in history could not teach history—unless it is at the university level. In other words, education is considered a field of study all by itself, the study of which will enable one to teach things he has not studied. We require of our teachers a knowledge of how to impart information; we do not require them to have a thorough grasp of that information. But mastering methods of teaching is not as difficult as electrical engineering, chemistry, or history. Consequently, departments of education tend to attract people who are having academic difficulty in other fields. And then we wonder at the dismal results! The truth of this generalization is not affected by those many well-qualified teachers who enter the system for admirable reasons.[11]

People of lesser caliber *are* attracted to an educational system where performance is not evaluated by the market. The market is insensitive to feelings, unkind to poor performance, and must therefore be avoided. So then we have a system of socialized education, which will tend toward mediocrity in education and excellence in bureaucratization. The problem will be exacerbated by the fact that such a system will have difficulty attracting excellent teachers to it because abilities are irrelevant to the goals of the system. So until the suggested reforms affect the heart of the system, which is government control over education, the reforms will not work.[12]

TWELVE

THE NEED FOR CLASSICAL AND CHRISTIAN EDUCATION: A SUMMARY

*H*ow far then have we come? Have we arrived at a truly Christian vision of what education ought to be?

We began with the recognition that education in America is in horrible shape. Never have we had so many resources spent on so many students with so little results. Not only is education in a bad way, it appears to be caught in a downward cycle. The more apparent the problems become, the more the education establishment thwarts calls for genuine reform. The cycle must be broken; we must make room for the Christian worldview in educating our children.

But not everyone wants to give up on the public schools. As the barrenness of humanistic thinking becomes more and more apparent, many come forward with suggestions for fertility treatments. In many cases, the suggested reforms are good ones. But unfortunately, they cannot work in the public sector. Private education is frequently the embodiment of these reforms, while public education, almost by definition, rejects them.

The Bible gives responsibility for education to the family, the God-ordained ministry of health, education and welfare. It is important to guard this assignment against well-intentioned encroachments from other institutions—even the church, or a private school, for example.

The Christian view of education takes into account that because there is a Creator God, the universe coheres. Consequently, knowledge about that universe coheres. This means that a unified curriculum is, *in principle*, possible. It is not necessary for the student to forget what he learned in science class while on his way to Bible class. The world is not fragmented; it is not a meaningless junk heap of unrelated particulars. In addition, we must consider the nature of man. Is the child basically good, ready and eager to learn? Or do all children of human parents have a sin problem? And where this problem exists, is education able to deal with it? Is education a savior? The Christian is required to say, "No." Our only Savior is Christ Jesus; all others are thieves and robbers.

But even though unified knowledge cannot save, it can be imparted in such a way that the student comes to love and understand it. Part of the understanding includes an understanding of the limitations of knowledge. Learning is received and appreciated for what it is, *and what it is not*. What enables a student to come to this understanding is the love the teacher has for the subject. Biblical love bestows loveliness.

Once we have worked out a distinctively Christian approach to education, we are still not done. A Christian school requires diligent thought and hard work in prayer. It is not enough to take whatever educational philosophy is currently about, add prayer and a Bible class, and somehow think that the result will be satisfactory. We want not only a Christian education; we want also a classical education. But in order for a thorough education to be established anywhere, the thinking must be radical. Radical thinking is not necessarily revolutionary thinking. *Radical* comes from the Latin root *radix*, which means "root." What are the roots of education in our Western civilization? Dorothy Sayers answered the question in her essay *The Lost Tools of Learning*. She applied the structure of the medieval pattern for education and found that it fit the development of young people very well indeed. The three parts of the *Trivium* are grammar, logic and rhetoric. The three stages children go through that correspond to the *Trivium* she labels as the Poll-parrot, Pert, and Poetic stages. We have sought to build our curriculum around this structure and have found that it works. But at the same time, a classical education involves more than a procedural outline. There is a certain necessary *history* to it.

We also saw that a rigorous education depends on factors outside the classroom as well. Some of these factors are how children are treated at home, how much TV they watch, what sort of music they listen to, and so on. Christian educators cannot solve all such problems, but they certainly should and must take them into account.

Because knowledge cannot save and because many have fallen

into the trap of thinking it can, some Christians have developed a spirit of anti-intellectualism. They have come to believe that true Christianity and true scholarship are incompatible. This conviction is buttressed with misunderstood passages of the Bible, along with a bitter memory of what a false scholarship has done to Christianity over the last 130 years.

Does the logic of all this require that parents home school? Not necessarily—no more than the Biblical requirement to feed our children requires us all to become farmers. Abdication of parental responsibility is possible even with home schooling. What is Biblically necessary? Parents must know what and how their children are being taught. The content and manner must be Biblical. This requires either home schooling or constant involvement with the private school. If the school is a good one, it will encourage such involvement. Otherwise, the private school is committing the same sin public schools are, only in the name of Christ.

CAN THIS ACTUALLY BE DONE?

Some may shrug and say that such a work as Logos is not possible in their community. Why even try? Such an attitude underestimates two things—the power of God and the power of ideas. Christian education is not a fad, nor is rigorous and successful Christian education a fluke. It is something that must of necessity accompany the expansion of Christ's kingdom. Consequently, thorough Christian education can go anywhere Christianity can. As we seek to be used by God in building that kingdom, we must exchange concepts and ideas as we learn from Scripture and one another—and from history.

There is continuity in history. Because God governs the universe, down to falling sparrows and fading hair, that continuity is *His*. He raises kings, and He deposes them. He turns the heart of the ruler in whatever direction He wishes (Proverbs 21:1). As far as history is concerned, there is no such thing as chance. But what is true of history must also be true of the history of education. Now one of the instruments used by God to govern men is the instrument of blessings and curses. "Blessed is the nation whose God is the Lord" (Psalm 33:12). A nation that repudiates the Lord is not under that blessing, and a nation that, as a matter of principle, excludes the light of God's Word from its system of education is a nation under a curse. Nations that honor God are honored by God. Nations that curse Him find that their curses fall back on their own heads.

We face disaster in education, both academic and moral, *because we have forgotten God*. It is impossible to expect a secularized system to do what can only be done under the blessing of God. And it is impudent to expect God to bless a secular system that refuses, as a matter of principle, to acknowledge Him in any way. ". . . in all your ways acknowledge Him, and He will make your paths straight" (Proverbs 3:6). Do we really want Him to straighten out our educational paths, while reserving the right to be officially agnostic? C. S. Lewis spoke of a ghastly simplicity that afflicts the modern mind. He wrote that we remove the organ and demand the function. We laugh at honor and are shocked to find traitors in our midst. We castrate and bid the geldings to be fruitful.[1] Night after night public school students study textbooks that scrupulously avoid any mention of Christianity. Day after day they go to school to have their values clarified. King Absolute is dead, long live the relatives!

But then the bills start coming due, and people become upset. Our schools are plagued with drugs, violence, assault, and other consequences of a permissive relativism. Academic proficiency is plummeting. But relativists want to pretend that their ethical system works. When evidence that it does not work starts to pile up, they also want to wonder why. But it is not logical to cut down the tree and demand the fruit at harvest. Our system of education is morally bankrupt (because the philosophy undergirding it is false), and the checks are starting to bounce. From a Biblical perspective, effective reform of such an educational system cannot be accomplished because reform can only be effective if it is blessed by God. In a pluralistic society, how can the God and Father of the Lord Jesus Christ be acknowledged in the public schools? And if He is ignored, dare we expect His blessing?

This general breakdown of morality and the failure of Christians to check it is an important problem for our schools—for an obvious reason. If there is not a disciplined morality in the schools, it will not be long before there is *no* discipline in the schools, moral or academic. A strict moral discipline is essential to the educational process. Indeed, many reformers have seen this and want a return to "traditional values." But the catch is that pragmatism is not a marching creed. When traditional morals are adopted for their utilitarian value, the foundation for true morals has been destroyed. We cannot turn the public schools around by trying to turn the kids into Judeo/Christians. From the Biblical perspective, morals aren't even *moral* when they are embraced for their side effects. In the Christian view, the truly moral thing is what is done for the glory of God. But at the same time, our schools are falling apart, and the disintegration of morality is part of the problem.

What should the Christian response be? Our children are the

only link between us and our descendants. If we are to have an impact on the future, the major means of doing so will be found in how we rear our children. Have we taught them to fear the Lord and to walk in the way He has required? Or have we turned them over for their education to those who do not fear God? Have we allowed someone else to send *their* message to the future? And will that message be blessed by God? When Jesus Christ gave His great commission to His apostles, He told them that He wanted the nations to be discipled. He did *not* say that He wanted a handful of Albanians, a smattering of Pakistanis, a remnant of Germans, and scores of North Americans. When the great Scottish Reformer John Knox prayed, he did not ask for enough Scots to enable him to get together a Bible study. He prayed for *Scotland*—and the Lord granted his request. Jesus said we were to disciple the nations, *teaching* them . . . (Matthew 28:16-20).

If we really begin to educate our children as the Bible requires, the future is hopeful for us and our children. If we do not, the future remains hopeful—but not for *us*. God is still God, and He remains in control. Christ is the ruler of the nations, regardless of what we do. But the consequences of both obedience and disobedience flow downstream. More than once in history, God has withdrawn His blessings from people who ceased to fear Him and given those blessings to those who worship and serve Him in everything. His word will go forth and it will not return empty; His word will be accomplished. As the wonderful Old Testament vision had it, the earth will be as full of the knowledge of the Lord as the waters cover the sea (Isaiah 11:9). Children *will* be taught in the Lord. The only question is whether *our* children will be in that number. The answer to that question is found in our obedience or lack of it. As we seek to obey God in this question of education, we need to remember what is at stake. It is *not* the purpose of God in history. That will be accomplished no matter what we do. What then, is at stake? It is nothing less than the blessing of God on us and our children.

THE LOST TOOLS OF LEARNING

Dorothy Sayers

QUALIFICATIONS

That I, whose experience of teaching is extremely limited, should presume to discuss education is a matter, surely, that calls for no apology. It is a kind of behavior to which the present climate of opinion is wholly favorable. Bishops air their opinions about economics; biologists about metaphysics; inorganic chemists about theology; the most irrelevant people are appointed to highly technical ministries; and plain, blunt men write to the papers to say that Epstein and Picasso do not know how to draw. Up to a certain point, and provided that the criticisms are made with a reasonable modesty, these activities are commendable. Too much specialization is not a good thing. There is also one excellent reason why the veriest amateur may feel entitled to have an opinion about education. For if we are not all professional teachers, we have all, at some time or other, been taught. Even if we learned nothing—perhaps in particular if we learned nothing—our contribution to the discussion may have a potential value.

I propose to deal with the subject of teaching, properly so-called. It is in the highest degree improbable that the reforms I propose will ever be carried into effect. Neither the parents, nor the training colleges, nor the examination boards, nor the boards of governors, nor the ministries of education would countenance them for a moment. For they amount to this: that if we are to produce a society of educated people, fitted to preserve their intellectual freedom amid the complex pressures of our modern society, we must turn back the wheel of progress some four or five hundred years, to the point at which education began to lose sight of its true object, towards the end of the Middle Ages.

Before you dismiss me with the appropriate phrase—reactionary, romantic, medievalist, *laudator temporis acti*, or whatever tag comes first to hand—I will ask you to consider one or two miscellaneous questions that hang about at the back, perhaps, of all our minds, and occasionally pop out to worry us.

SOME DISQUIETING QUESTIONS

When we think about the remarkable early age at which the young men went up to the university in, let us say, Tudor times, and thereafter were held fit to assume responsibility for the conduct of their own affairs, are we altogether comfortable about that artificial prolongation of intellectual childhood and adolescence into the years of physical maturity which is so marked in our day? To postpone the acceptance of responsibility to a late date brings with it a number of psychological complications which, while they may interest the psychiatrist, are scarcely beneficial either to the individual or to society. The stock argument in favor of postponing the school leaving-age and prolonging the period of education generally is that there is now so much more to learn than there was in the Middle Ages. This is partly true, but not wholly. The modern boy and girl are certainly taught more subjects—but does that always mean that they actually know more?

Has it ever struck you as odd, or unfortunate, that today, when the proportion of literacy throughout Western Europe is higher than it has ever been, people should have become susceptible to the influence of advertisement and mass propaganda to an extent hitherto unheard-of and unimagined? Do you put this down to the mere mechanical fact that the press and the radio and so on have made propaganda much easier to distribute over a wide area? Or do you sometimes have an uneasy suspicion that the product of modern educational methods is less good than he or she might be at disentangling fact from opinion and the proven from the plausible?

Have you ever, in listening to a debate among adult and presumably responsible people, been fretted by the extraordinary inability of the average debater to speak to the question, or to meet and refute the arguments of speakers on the other side? Or have you ever pondered upon the extremely high incidence of irrelevant matter which crops up at committee meetings, and upon the very great rarity of persons capable of acting as chairmen of committees? And when you think of this, and think that most of our public affairs are settled by debates and committees, have you ever felt a certain sinking of the heart?

Have you ever followed a discussion in the newspapers or elsewhere and noticed how frequently writers fail to define the terms they use? Or how often, if one man does define his terms, another will assume in his reply that he was using the terms in precisely the opposite sense to that in which he has already defined them?

Have you ever been faintly troubled by the amount of slipshod syntax going about? And if so, are you troubled because it is inelegant or because it may lead to dangerous misunderstanding?

Do you ever find that young people, when they have left school, not only forget most of what they have learned (that is only to be expected) but forget also, or betray that they have never really known, how to tackle a new subject for themselves? Are you often bothered by coming across grown-up men and women who seem unable to distinguish between a book that is sound, scholarly and properly documented, and one that is to any trained eye, very conspicuously none of these things? Or who cannot handle a library catalogue? Or who, when faced with a book of reference, betray a curious inability to extract from it the passages relevant to the particular question which interests them?

Do you often come across people for whom, all their lives, a "subject" remains a "subject," divided by watertight bulkheads from all other "subjects," so that they experience very great difficulty in making an immediate mental connection between, let us say, algebra and detective fiction, sewage disposal and the price of salmon—or, more generally, between such spheres of knowledge as philosophy and economics, or chemistry and art?

EXAMPLES

Are you occasionally perturbed by the things written by adult men and women for adult men and women to read?

We find a well-known biologist writing in a weekly paper to the effect that: "It is an argument against the existence of a Creator" (I think he put it more strongly; but since I have, most unfortunately, mislaid the reference, I will put his claim at its lowest)—"an argument against the existence of a Creator that the same kind of variations which are produced by natural selection can be produced at

will by stock-breeders." One might feel tempted to say that it is
rather an argument *for* the existence of a Creator. Actually, of
course, it is neither; all it proves is that the same material causes
(recombination of the chromosomes by cross-breeding and so forth)
are sufficient to account for all observed variations—just as the various combinations of the same thirteen semitones are materially
sufficient to account for Beethoven's Moonlight Sonata and the
noise the cat makes by walking on the keys. But the cat's performance neither proves nor disproves the existence of Beethoven; and
all that is proved by the biologist's argument is that he was unable
to distinguish between a material and a final cause.

Here is a sentence from no less academic a source than a front
page article in the [London] *Times Literary Supplement*:

> The Frenchman, Alfred Epinas, pointed out that certain species
> (e.g., ants and wasps) can only face the horrors of life and death
> in association.

I do not know what the Frenchman actually did say; what the
Englishman says he said is patently meaningless. We cannot know
whether life holds any horror for the ant, nor in what sense the isolated wasp which you kill upon the window pane can be said to
"face" or not to "face" the horrors of death. The subject of the article is mass behavior in *man*; and the human motives have been
unobtrusively transferred from the main proposition to the supporting instance. Thus the argument, in effect, assumes what it sets
out to prove—a fact which would become immediately apparent if
it were presented in a formal syllogism. This is only a small and hap-
hazard example of a vice which pervades whole books—particularly
books written by men of science on metaphysical subjects.

Another quotation from the same issue of the T.L.S. comes in
fittingly here to wind up this random collection of disquieting
thoughts—this time from a review of Sir Richard Livingstone's
Some Tasks for Education:

> More than once the reader is reminded of the value of an inten-
> sive study of at least one subject, so as to learn "the meaning of
> knowledge" and what precision and persistence is needed to
> attain it. Yet there is elsewhere full recognition of the distressing
> fact that a man may be master in one field and show no better
> judgment than his neighbor anywhere else; he remembers what
> he has learned, but forgets altogether how he learned it.

I would draw your attention particularly to that last sentence, which offers an explanation of what the writer rightly calls the "distressing fact" that the intellectual skills bestowed upon us by our education are not readily transferable to subjects other than those in which we acquired them: "he remembers what he has learned, but forgets altogether how he learned it."

THE ART OF LEARNING

Is it not the great defect of our education today that although we often succeed in teaching our pupils "subjects," we fail lamentably on the whole in teaching them how to think? They learn everything, except the art of learning. It is as though we had taught a child, mechanically and by rule of thumb, to play "The Harmonious Blacksmith" upon the piano, but had never taught him the scale or how to read music; so that, having memorized "The Harmonious Blacksmith," he still had not the faintest notion how to proceed from that to tackle "The Last Rose of Summer." Why do I say, "As though"? In certain of the arts and crafts we sometimes do precisely this—requiring a child to "express himself" in paint before we teach him how to handle the colors and the brush. There is a school of thought which believes this to be the right way to set about the job. But observe—it is not the way in which a trained craftsman will go about to teach himself a new medium. *He*, having learned by experience the best way to economize labour and take the thing by the right end, will start off by doodling about on an odd piece of material, in order to "give himself the feel of the tool."

Let us now look at the mediaeval scheme of education—the syllabus of the schools. It does not matter, for the moment, whether it was devised for small children or for older students; or how long people were supposed to take over it. What matters is the light it throws upon what the men of the Middle Ages supposed to be the object and the right order of the educative process.

THE MEDIAEVAL SYLLABUS

The syllabus was divided into two parts: the Trivium and Quadrivium. The second part—the Quadrivium—consisted of "subjects," and need not for the moment concern us. The interesting thing for us is the composition of the Trivium, which preceded the Quadrivium and was the preliminary discipline for it. It consisted of three parts: grammar, dialectic, and rhetoric, in that order.

Now the first thing we notice is that two at any rate of these "subjects" are not what we should call "subjects" at all: they are only methods of dealing with subjects. Grammar indeed is a "subject" in the sense that it does mean definitely learning a language—at that period it meant learning Latin. But language itself is simply the medium in which thought is expressed. The whole of the Trivium was in fact intended to teach the pupil the proper use of the tools of learning before he began to apply them to "subjects" at all. First, he learned a language: not just how to order a meal in a foreign language, but the structure of language—*any* language—and hence of language itself—what it was, how it was put together and how it worked. Secondly, he learned how to use language: how to define his terms and make accurate statements, how to construct an argument and how to detect fallacies in argument (his own arguments and other people's). Dialectic, that is to say, embraced logic and disputation. Thirdly, he learned to express himself in language: how to say what he had to say elegantly and persuasively. At this point, any tendency to express himself windily or to use his eloquence so as to make the worse appear the better reason would, no doubt, be restrained by his previous teaching in dialectic. If not, his teacher and his fellow pupils, trained along the same lines, would be quick to point out where he was wrong; for it was they whom he had to seek to persuade. At the end of his course, he was required to compose a thesis upon some theme set by his masters or chosen by himself, and afterwards to defend his thesis against the criticism of the faculty. By this time he would have learned—or woe betide him—not merely to write an essay on paper, but to speak audibly and intelligibly from a platform and to use his wits quickly when heckled. The heckling, moreover, would not consist solely of offensive personalities or of irrelevant queries about what Julius Caesar said in 55 B.C.—though no doubt mediaeval dialectic was enlivened in practice by plenty of such primitive repartee. But there would also be questions, cogent and shrewd, from those who had already run the gauntlet of debate, or were making ready to run it.

It is, of course, quite true that bits and pieces of the mediaeval tradition still linger, or have been revived, in the ordinary school syllabus of today. Some knowledge of grammar is still required when learning a foreign language—perhaps I should say, "is again required"; for during my own lifetime we passed through a phase when the teaching of declensions and conjugations was considered rather reprehensible, and it was considered better to pick these things up as we went along. School debating societies flourish; essays are written; the necessity for "self expression" is

stressed, and perhaps even over-stressed. But these activities are cultivated more or less in detachment, as belonging to the special subjects in which they are pigeon-holed rather than as forming one
coherent scheme of mental training to which all "subjects" stand
in subordinate relation. "Grammar" belongs especially to the "subject" of foreign languages, and essay-writing to the "subject" called
"English"; while dialectic has become almost entirely divorced
from the rest of the curriculum, and is frequently practised unsys-
tematically and out of school hours as a separate exercise, only very
loosely related to the main business of learning. Taken by and large,
the great difference of emphasis between the two conceptions holds
good: modern education concentrates on *teaching subjects*, leaving
the method of thinking, arguing, and expressing one's conclusions
to be picked up by the scholar as he goes along; mediaeval education concentrated on first *forging and learning to handle the tools
of learning*, using whatever subject came handy as a piece of material on which to doodle until the use of the tool became second
nature.

        "Subjects" of some kind there must be, of course. One cannot
learn the use of a tool by merely waving it in the air; neither can one
learn the theory of grammar without learning an actual language,
or learn to argue and orate without speaking about something in
particular. The debating subjects of the Middle Ages were drawn
largely from Theology, or from the Ethics and History of Antiquity.
Often, indeed, they became stereotyped, especially towards the end
of the period; and the far-fetched and wire-drawn absurdities of
scholastic argument fretted Milton and provide food for merriment
even to this day. Whether they were in themselves any more hack-
neyed and trivial than the usual subjects set nowadays for "essay-
writing" I should not like to say: we may ourselves grow a little
weary of "A Day in My Holidays," "What I Should Like to Do
When I Leave School," and all the rest of it. But most of the merriment is misplaced, because the aim and object of the debating thesis has by now been lost sight of.

ANGELS AND NEEDLES

A glib speaker in the Brains Trust once entertained his audience (and
reduced the late Charles Williams to helpless rage) by asserting that
in the Middle Ages it was a matter of faith to know how many
archangels could dance on the point of a needle. I need not say, I
hope, that it never was a "matter of faith"; it was simply a debating
exercise, whose set subject was the nature of angelic substance; were

angels material, and if so, did they occupy space? The answer usually adjudged correct is, I believe, that angels are pure intelligences, not material, but limited, so that they have location in space but not extension. An analogy might be drawn from human thought, which is similarly nonmaterial and similarly limited. Thus, if your thought is concentrated upon one thing—say, the point of a needle—it is located there in the sense that it is not elsewhere; but although it is "there," it occupies no space there, and there is nothing to prevent an infinite number of different people's thoughts being concentrated upon the same needle-point at the same time. The proper *subject* of the argument is thus seen to be the distinction between location and extension in space; the *matter* on which the argument is exercised happens to be the nature of angels (although, as we have seen, it might equally well have been something else); the practical lesson to be drawn from the argument is not to use words like "there" in a loose and unscientific way, without specifying whether you mean "located there" or "occupying space there." Scorn in plenty has been poured out upon the mediaeval passion for hair-splitting; but when we look at the shameless abuse made, in print and on the platform, of controversial expressions with shifting and ambiguous connotations, we may feel it in our hearts to wish that every reader and hearer had been so defensively armored by his education as to be able to cry: *Distinguo*.

UNARMED AND UNEQUIPPED

For we let our young men and women go out unarmed in a day when armor was never so necessary. By teaching them to read, we have left them at the mercy of the printed word. By the invention of the film and the radio, we have made certain that no aversion to reading shall secure them from the incessant battery of words, words, words. They do not know what the words mean; they do not know how to ward them off or blunt their edge or fling them back; they are a prey to words in their emotions instead of being the masters of them in their intellects. We who were scandalized in 1940 when men were sent to fight armored tanks with rifles, are not scandalized when young men and women are sent into the world to fight mass propaganda with a smattering of "subjects"; and when whole classes and whole nations become hypnotized by the arts of the spellbinder, we have the impudence to be astonished. We dole out lip-service to the importance of education—lip-service and, just occasionally, a little grant of money; we postpone the school leaving-age, and plan to build bigger and better schools; the teachers slave conscientiously in and out of school hours, till responsibility becomes a burden and a nightmare; and yet, as I believe, all this devoted effort is largely frustrated, because we have lost the tools of learning, and in their absence can only make a botched and piece-meal job of it.

What, then, are we to do? We cannot go back to the Middle Ages. That is a cry to which we have become accustomed. We cannot go back—or can we? *Distinguo*. I should like every term in that proposition defined. Does "Go back" mean a retrogression in time, or the revision of an error? The first is clearly impossible *per se*; the second is a thing which wise men do every day. "Cannot"—does this mean that our behavior is determined by some irreversible cosmic mechanism, or merely that such an action would be very difficult in view of the opposition it would provoke? "The Middle Ages"— obviously the twentieth century is not and cannot be the fourteenth; but if "the Middle Ages" is, in this context, simply a picturesque phrase denoting a particular educational theory, there seems to be no *a priori* reason why we should not "go back" to it—with modifications—as we have already "gone back," with modifications, to, let us say, the idea of playing Shakespeare's plays as he wrote them, and not in the "modernized" versions of Cibber and Garrick, which once seemed to be the latest thing in theatrical progress.

Let us amuse ourselves by imagining that such progressive retrogression is possible. Let us make a clean sweep of all educational authorities, and furnish ourselves with a nice little school of boys and girls whom we may experimentally equip for the intellectual conflict along lines chosen by ourselves. We will endow them with exceptionally docile parents; we will staff our school with teachers who are themselves perfectly familiar with the aims and methods of the Trivium; we will have our buildings and staff large enough to allow our classes to be small enough for adequate handling; and we will postulate a Board of Examiners willing and qualified to test the products we turn out. Thus prepared, we will attempt to sketch out a syllabus—a modern Trivium "with modifications"; and we will see where we get to.

But first: what age shall the children be? Well, if one is to educate them on novel lines, it will be better that they should have nothing to unlearn; besides, one cannot begin a good thing too early, and the Trivium is by its nature not learning, but a preparation for learning. We will therefore "catch 'em young," requiring only of our pupils that they shall be able to read, write and cipher.

THE THREE STAGES

My views about child psychology are, I admit, neither orthodox nor enlightened. Looking back upon myself (since I am the child I know best and the only child I can pretend to know from inside) I recognize in myself three stages of development. These, in a rough-and-ready fashion, I will call the Poll-parrot, the Pert, and the Poetic—the latter coinciding, approximately, with the onset of puberty. The Poll-parrot stage is the one in which learning by heart is easy and, on the whole, pleasurable; whereas reasoning is difficult and, on the whole, little relished. At this age one readily memorizes the shapes and appearances of things; one likes to recite the number-plates of cars; one rejoices in the chanting of rhymes and the rumble and thunder of unintelligible polysyllables; one enjoys the mere accumulation of things. The Pert Age, which follows upon this (and, naturally, overlaps it to some extent) is only too familiar to all who have to do with children: it is characterized by contradicting, answering-back, liking to "catch people out" (especially one's elders) and the propounding of conundrums (especially the kind with a nasty verbal catch in them). Its nuisance-value is extremely high. It usually sets in about the Lower Fourth. The Poetic Age is popularly known as the "difficult" age. It is self-centered; it yearns to express itself; it rather specializes in being misunderstood; it is restless and tries to achieve independence; and, with good luck and good guidance, it should show the beginnings of creativeness, a reaching-out towards a synthesis of what it already knows, and a deliberate eagerness to know and do some one thing in preference to all others. Now it seems to me that the lay-out of the Trivium adapts itself with a singular appropriateness to these three ages: grammar to the Poll-parrot, dialectic to the Pert, and rhetoric to the Poetic age.

Let us begin, then, with grammar. This, in practice, means the grammar of some language in particular; and it must be an inflected language. The grammatical structure of an uninflected language is far too analytical to be tackled by any one without previous practice in dialectic. Moreover, the inflected languages interpret the uninflected, whereas the uninflected are of little use in interpreting the inflected. I will say at once, quite firmly, that the best grounding for education is the Latin grammar. I say this, not because Latin is traditional and mediaeval, but simply because even a rudimentary knowledge of Latin cuts down the labour and pains of learning almost any other subject by at least 50 percent. It is the key to the vocabulary and structure of all the Romance languages and to the structure of all the Teutonic languages, as well as to the technical vocabulary of all the sciences and to the literature of the entire Mediterranean civilization, together with all its historical documents.

Those whose pedantic preference for a living language persuades them to deprive their pupils of all these advantages might substitute Russian, whose grammar is still more primitive. (The verb is complicated by a number of "aspects"—and I rather fancy that it enjoys three complete voices and a couple of extra aorists—but I may be thinking of Basque or Sanskrit.) Russian is, of course, helpful with the other Slav dialects. There is something also to be said for classical Greek. But my own choice is Latin. Having thus pleased the Classicists, I will proceed to horrify them by adding that I do not think it either wise or necessary to cramp the ordinary pupil upon the Procrustean bed of the Augustan Age, with its highly elaborate and artificial verse-forms and oratory. The post-classical and mediaeval Latin, which was a living language down to the end of the Renaissance, is easier and in some ways livelier, both in syntax and rhythm; and a study of it helps to dispel the widespread notion that learning and literature came to a full-stop when Christ was born and only woke up again at the Dissolution of the Monasteries.

However, I am running ahead too fast. We are still in the grammatical stage. Latin should be begun as early as possible—at a time when inflected speech seems no more astonishing than any other phenomenon in an astonishing world; and when the chanting of "*amo, amas, amat*" is as ritually agreeable to the feelings as the chanting of "eeny, meeny, miney, mo."

During this age we must, of course, exercise the mind on other things besides Latin grammar. Observation and memory are the faculties most lively at this period; and if we are to learn a contemporary foreign language we should begin now, before the facial and mental muscles become rebellious to strange intonations. Spoken French or German can be practised alongside the grammatical discipline of the Latin.

THE FUNCTION OF MEMORY

In *English*, the verse and prose can be learned by heart, and the pupil's memory should be stored with stories of every kind—classical myth, European legend, and so forth. I do not think that the Classical stories and masterpieces of ancient literature should be made the vile bodies on which to practise the technics of grammar— that was a fault of mediaeval education which we need not perpetuate. The stories can be enjoyed and remembered in English, and related to their origin at a subsequent stage. Recitation aloud should be practised—individually or in chorus; for we must not forget that we are laying the ground work for disputation and rhetoric.

The grammar of *History* should consist, I think, of dates, events, anecdotes, and personalities. A set of dates to which one can peg all later historical knowledge is of enormous help later on in establishing the perspective of history. It does not greatly matter *which* dates: those of the Kings of England will do very nicely, provided that they are accompanied by pictures of costume, architecture, and all "every-day things," so that the mere mention of a date calls up a strong visual presentment of the whole period.

Geography will similarly be presented in its factual aspect, with maps, natural features and visual presentment of customs, costumes, flora, fauna and so on; and I believe myself that the discredited and old-fashioned memorizing of a few capital cities, rivers, mountain ranges, etc., does not harm. Stamp-collecting may be encouraged.

Science, in the Poll-parrot period, arranges itself naturally and easily around collections—the identifying and naming of specimens and, in general, the kind of thing that used to be called "natural history," or, still more charmingly, "natural philosophy." To know the names and properties of things is, at this age, a satisfaction in itself: to recognize a devil's coach-horse at sight, and assure one's foolish elders that, in spite of its appearance, it does not sting; to be able to pick out Cassiopeia and the Pleiades, and possibly even to know who Cassiopeia and the Pleiades were; to be aware that a whale is not a fish, and a bat not a bird—all these things give a pleasant sensation of superiority; while to know a ring-snake from an adder or a poisonous from an edible toadstool is a kind of knowledge that has also a practical value.

The grammar of *Mathematics* begins, of course, with the multiplication table, which, if not learned now, will never be learned with pleasure; and with the recognition of geometrical shapes and the grouping of numbers. These exercises lead naturally to the doing of simple sums in arithmetic; and if the pupil shows a bent that way, a facility acquired at this stage is all to the good. More complicated mathematical processes may, and perhaps should, be postponed, for reasons which will presently appear.

So far (except, of course, for the Latin), our curriculum contains nothing that departs very far from common practice. The difference will be felt rather in the attitude of the teachers, who must look upon all these activities less as "subjects" in themselves than as a gathering-together of *material* for use in the next part of the Trivium. What that material actually is, is only of secondary importance; but it is as well that anything and everything which can usefully be committed to memory should be memorized at this period, whether it is immediately intelligible or not. The modern tendency is to try and force rational explanations on a child's mind at too early an age. Intelligent questions, spontaneously asked, should, of course, receive an immediate and rational answer; but it is a great mistake to suppose that a child cannot readily enjoy and remember things that are beyond its power to analyze—particularly if those things have a strong imaginative appeal (as, for example, *Kubla Khan*), an attractive jingle (like some of the memory-rhymes for Latin genders), or an abundance of rich, resounding polysyllables.

THEOLOGY: THE MISTRESS-SCIENCE

This reminds me of the grammar of *Theology*. I shall add it to the curriculum, because Theology is the Mistress-science, without which the whole educational structure will necessarily lack its final synthesis. Those who disagree about this will remain content to leave their pupils' education still full of loose ends. This will matter rather less than it might, since by the time that the tools of learning have been forged the student will be able to tackle Theology for himself, and will probably insist upon doing so and making sense of it. Still, it is as well to have this matter also handy and ready for the reason to work upon. At the grammatical age, therefore, we should become acquainted with story of God and man in outline—i.e. the Old and New Testaments presented as parts of a single narrative of Creation, Rebellion, and Redemption—and also with "the Creed, the Lord's Prayer and the Ten Commandments." At this stage, it does not matter nearly so much that these things should be fully understood as that they should be known and remembered. Remember, it is material that we are collecting.

It is difficult to say at what age, precisely, we should pass from the first to the second part of the Trivium. Generally speaking, the answer is: so soon as the pupil shows himself disposed to Pertness and interminable argument (or, as a school-master correspondent of mine more elegantly puts it: "When the capacity for abstract thought begins to manifest itself"). For as, in the first part, the master-faculties are observation and memory, so in the second, the master-faculty is the discursive reason. In the first, the exercise to which the rest of the material was, as it were, keyed, was the Latin grammar; in the second the key-exercise will be formal logic. It is here that our curriculum shows its first sharp divergence from modern standards. The disrepute into which formal logic has fallen is entirely unjustified; and its neglect is the root cause of nearly all those disquieting symptoms which we may note in the modern intellectual constitution. Logic has been discredited, partly because we have fallen into a habit of supposing that we are conditioned almost entirely by the intuitive and the unconscious. There is no time now to argue whether this is true; I will content myself with observing that to neglect the proper training of the reason is the best possible way to make it true, and to ensure the supremacy of the intuitive, irrational and unconscious elements in our make-up. A secondary cause for the disfavor into which formal logic has fallen is the belief that it is entirely based upon universal assumptions that are either unprovable or tautological. This is not true. Not all universal propositions are of this kind. But even if they were, it would make no difference, since every syllogism whose major premise is in the form "All A is B" can be recast in hypothetical form. Logic is the art of arguing correctly: "If A, then B"; the method is not invalidated by the hypothetical character of A. Indeed, the practical utility of formal logic today lies not so much in the establishment of positive conclusions as in the prompt detection and exposure of invalid inference.

THE RELATION TO DIALECTIC

Let us now quickly review our material and see how it is to be related to dialectic. On the *Language* side, we shall now have our vocabulary and morphology at our finger-tips; henceforward we can concentrate more particularly on syntax and analysis (i.e., the logical construction of speech) and the history of Language (i.e., how we came to arrange our speech as we do in order to convey our thoughts).

Our reading will proceed from narrative and lyric to essays, argument and criticism, and the pupil will learn to try his own hand at writing this kind of thing. Many lessons—on whatever subject—will take the form of debates; and the place of individual or choral recitation will be taken by dramatic performances, with special attention to plays in which an argument is stated in dramatic form.

Mathematics—algebra, geometry, and the more advanced kind of arithmetic—will now enter into the syllabus and take its place as what it really is: not a separate "subject" but a sub-department of logic. It is neither more nor less than the rule of the syllogism in its particular application to number and measurement, and should be taught as such, instead of being, for some, a dark mystery, and for others, a special revelation, neither illuminating, nor illuminated by any other part of knowledge.

History, aided by a simple system of ethics derived from the grammar of Theology, will provide much suitable material for discussion; was the behavior of this statesman justified? What was the effect of such an enactment? What are the arguments for and against this or that form of government? We shall thus get an introduction to constitutional history—a subject meaningless to the young child, but of absorbing interest to those who are prepared to argue and debate. *Theology* itself will furnish material for argument about conduct and morals; and should have its scope extended by a simplified course of dogmatic theology (i.e. the rational structure of Christian thought), clarifying the relations between the dogma and the ethics, and lending itself to that application of ethical principles in particular instances which is properly called casuistry. *Geography* and the *Sciences* will all likewise provide material for dialectic.

THE WORLD AROUND

But above all, we must not neglect the material which is so abundant in the pupils' own daily life. There is a delightful passage in Leslie Paul's *The Living Hedge* which tells how a number of small boys enjoyed themselves for days arguing about an extraordinary shower of rain which had fallen in their town—a shower so localized that it left one half of the main street wet and the other dry. Could one, they argued, properly say that it had rained that day *on* or *over* the town or only *in* the town? How many drops of water were required to constitute rain? and so on. Argument about this led on to a host of similar problems about rest and motion, sleep and waking, *est* and *non est*, and the infinitesimal division of time. The whole passage is an admirable example of the spontaneous development of the ratiocinative faculty and the natural and proper thirst of the awakening reason for definition of terms and exactness of statement. All events are food for such an appetite. An umpire's decision; the degree to which one may transgress the spirit of a regulation without being trapped by the letter; on such questions as these, children are born casuists, and their natural propensity only needs to be developed and trained—and, especially, brought into an intelligible relationship with events in the grown-up world. The newspapers are full of good material for such exercises: legal decisions, on the one hand, in cases where the cause at issue is not too abstruse; on the other, fallacious reasoning and muddle-headed argument, with which the correspondence columns of certain papers one could name are abundantly stocked.

PERT CRITICISM

Wherever the matter for dialectic is found, it is, of course, highly important that attention should be focused upon the beauty and economy of a fine demonstration or a well-turned argument, lest veneration should wholly die. Criticism must not be merely destructive; though at the same time both teacher and pupils must be ready to detect fallacy, slipshod reasoning, ambiguity, irrelevance and redundancy, and to pounce upon them like rats.

This is the moment when precis-writing may be usefully undertaken; together with such exercises as the writing of an essay, and the reduction of it, when written, by 25 or 50 percent.

It will doubtless be objected that to encourage young persons at the Pert Age to browbeat, correct, and argue with their elders will render them perfectly intolerable. My answer is that children of that age are intolerable anyhow; and that their natural argumentativeness may just as well be canalised to good purpose as allowed to run away into the sands. It may, indeed, be rather less obtrusive at home if it is disciplined in school; and, anyhow, elders who have abandoned the wholesome principle that children should be seen and not heard have no one to blame but themselves. The teachers, to be sure, will have to mind their step, or they may get more than they bargained for. All children sit in judgment on their masters; and if the Chaplain's sermon or the Headmistress's annual Speech-day address should by any chance afford an opening for the point of the critical wedge, that wedge will go home the more forcibly under the weight of the Dialectical hammer, wielded by a practised hand. That is why I said that the teachers themselves would have to have undergone the discipline of the Trivium before they set out to impose it on their charges.

Once again: the contents of the syllabus at this stage may be anything you like. The "subjects" supply material; but they are all to be regarded as mere grist for the mental mill to work upon. The pupils should be encouraged to go and forage for their own information, and so guided towards the proper use of libraries and books of reference, and shown how to tell which sources are authoritative and which are not.

THE IMAGINATION

Towards the close of this stage, the pupils will probably be beginning to discover for themselves that their knowledge and experience are insufficient, and that their trained intelligences need a great deal more material to chew upon. The imagination—usually dormant during the Pert Age—will reawaken, and prompt them to suspect the limitations of logic and reason. This means that they are passing into the Poetic Age and are ready to embark on the study of rhetoric. The doors of the storehouse of knowledge should now be thrown open for them to browse about as they will. The things once learned by rote will now be seen in new contexts; the things once coldly analyzed can now be brought together to form a new synthesis; here and there a sudden insight will bring about that most exciting of all discoveries: the realization that a truism is true.

THE STUDY OF RHETORIC

It is difficult to map out any general syllabus for the study of rhetoric: a certain freedom is demanded. In literature, appreciation should be again allowed to take the lead over destructive criticism; and self-expression in writing can go forward, with its tools now sharpened to cut clean and observe proportion. Any child that already shows a disposition to specialize should be given his head: for, when the use of the tools has been well and truly learned, it is available for any study whatever. It would be well, I think, that each pupil should learn to do one, or two, subjects really well, while taking a few classes in subsidiary subjects so as to keep his mind open to the inter-relations of all knowledge. Indeed, at this stage, our difficulty will be to keep "subjects" apart; for as dialectic will have shown all branches of learning to be inter-related, so rhetoric will tend to show that all knowledge is one. To show this, and show why it is so, is pre-eminently the task of the Mistress-science. But whether Theology is studied or not, we should at least insist that children who seem inclined to specialize on the mathematical and scientific side should be obliged to attend some lessons in the humanities and *vice versa*. At this stage also, the Latin grammar, having done its work, may be dropped for those who prefer to carry on their language studies on the modern side; while those who are likely never to have any great use or aptitude for mathematics might also be allowed to rest, more or less, upon their oars. Generally speaking: whatsoever is *mere* apparatus may now be allowed to fall into the background, while the trained mind is gradually prepared for specialization in the "subjects" which, when the Trivium is completed, it should be perfectly well equipped to tackle on its own. The final synthesis of the Trivium—the presentation and public defence of the thesis should be restored in some form; perhaps as a kind of "leaving examination" during the last term at school.

The scope of rhetoric depends also on whether the pupil is to be turned out into the world at the age of sixteen, or whether he is to proceed to public school and/or university. Since, really, rhetoric should be taken at about fourteen, the first category of pupil should study grammar from about nine to eleven, and dialectic from twelve to fourteen; his last two school years would then be devoted to rhetoric, which, in his case, would be of a fairly practical career. A pupil of the second category would finish his dialectical course in his Preparatory School, and take rhetoric during his first two years at his Public School. At sixteen, he would be ready to start upon those "subjects" which are proposed for his later study at the university; and this part of his education will correspond to the mediaeval Quadrivium. What this amounts to is that the ordinary pupil, whose formal education ends at sixteen, will take the Trivium only; whereas scholars will take both Trivium and Quadrivium.

THE UNIVERSITY? AT SIXTEEN?

Is the Trivium, then, a sufficient education for life? Properly taught, I believe that it should be. At the end of dialectic, the children will probably seem to be far behind their coevals brought up on old-fashioned "modern" methods, so far as detailed knowledge of specific subjects is concerned. But after the age of fourteen they should be able to overhaul the others hand over fist. Indeed, I am not at all sure that a pupil thoroughly proficient in the Trivium would not be fit to proceed immediately to the university at the age of sixteen, thus proving himself the equal of his mediaeval counterpart, whose precocity often appears to us so astonishing and unaccountable. This, to be sure, would make hay of the public-school system, and disconcert the universities very much—it would, for example, make quite a different thing of the Oxford and Cambridge boat-race. But I am not now considering the feelings of academic bodies: I am concerned only with the proper training of the mind to encounter and deal with the formidable mass of undigested problems presented to it by the modern world. For the tools of learning are the same, in any and every subject; and the person who knows how to use them will, at any age, get the mastery of a new subject in half the time and with a quarter of the effort expended by the person who has not the tools at his command. To learn six subjects without remembering how they were learned does nothing to ease the approach to a seventh; to have learned and remembered the art of learning makes the approach to every subject an open door.

It is clear that the successful teaching of this neo-mediaeval curriculum will depend even more than usual upon the working together of the whole teaching staff towards a common purpose. Since no subject is considered as an end in itself, any kind of rivalry in the staff-room will be sadly out of place. The fact that a pupil is unfortunately obliged, for some reason, to miss the history period on Fridays, or the Shakespeare class on Tuesdays, or even to omit a whole subject in favour of some other subject, must not be allowed to cause any heart-burnings—the essential is that he should acquire the method of learning in whatever medium suits him best. If human nature suffers under this blow to one's professional pride in one's own subject, there is comfort in the thought that the end-of-term examination results will not be affected; for the papers will be so arranged as to be an examination in method, by whatever means.

I will add that it is highly important that every teacher should, for his or her own sake, be qualified and required to teach in all three parts of the Trivium; otherwise the Masters of dialectic, especially, might find their minds hardening into a permanent adolescence. For this reason, teachers in Preparatory Schools should also take rhetoric classes in the Public Schools to which they are attached; or, if they are not so attached, then by arrangement in other schools in the same neighborhood. Alternatively, a few preliminary classes in rhetoric might be taken in Preparatory Schools from the age of thirteen onwards.

SQUANDERING EDUCATIONAL CAPITAL

Before concluding these necessarily very sketchy suggestions, I ought to say why I think it necessary, in these days, to go back to a discipline which we had discarded. The truth is that for the last 300 years or so we have been living upon our educational capital. The post-Renaissance world, bewildered and excited by the profusion of new "subjects" offered to it, broke away from the old discipline (which had, indeed, become sadly dull and stereotyped in its practical application) and imagined that henceforward it could, as it were, disport itself happily in its new and extended Quadrivium without passing through the Trivium. But the scholastic tradition, though broken and maimed, still lingered in the public schools and universities: Milton, however much he protested against it, was formed by it—the debate of the Fallen Angels, and the disputation of Abdiel with Satan have the tool-marks of the Schools upon them, and might, incidentally, profitably figure as a set passage for our dialectical studies. Right down to the nineteenth century, our public affairs were mostly managed, and our books and journals were for the most part written, by people brought up in homes, and trained in places, where that tradition was still alive in the memory and almost in the blood. Just so, many people today who are atheist or agnostic in religion, are governed in their conduct by a code of Christian ethics which is so rooted in their unconscious assumptions that it never occurs to them to question it.

NEGLECTED ROOTS

But one cannot live on capital for ever. A tradition, however firmly rooted, if it is never watered, though it dies hard, yet in the end it dies. And today a great number—perhaps the majority—of the men and women who handle our affairs, write our books and our newspapers, carry out research, present our plays and our films, speak from our platforms and pulpits—yes, and who educate our young people, have never, even in a lingering traditional memory, undergone the scholastic discipline. Less and less do the children who come to be educated bring any of that tradition with them. We have lost the tools of learning—the axe and the wedge, the hammer and the saw, the chisel and the plane—that were so adaptable to all tasks. Instead of them, we have merely a set of complicated jigs, each of which will do but one task and no more, and in using which eye and hand receive no training, so that no man ever sees the work as a whole or "looks to the end of the work." What use is it to pile task on task and prolong the days of labour, if at the close the chief object is left unattained? It is not the fault of the teachers—they work only too hard already. The combined folly of a civilization that has forgotten its own roots is forcing them to shore up the tottering weight of an educational structure that is built upon sand. They are doing for their pupils the work which the pupils themselves ought to do. For the sole end of education is simply this: to teach men how to learn for themselves; and whatever instruction fails to do this is effort spent in vain.

Paper read by Dorothy Sayers at Oxford University in 1947. Reprinted with the kind permission of Methuen & Co., Ltd., (METHUEN LONDON), a division of Routledge, Chapman, and Hall, Ltd. Minor editing changes were made for the sake of the American reader.

LOGOS SCHOOL CURRICULUM MATERIAL
A Classical and Christ-centered Education

CHRIST-CENTERED

In all its levels, programs, and teaching, Logos School seeks to:
   A. Teach all subjects as parts of an integrated whole with the Scriptures at the center (2 Timothy 3:16-17);
   B. Provide a clear model of the Biblical Christian life through our staff and board (Matthew 22:37-40);
   C. Encourage every child to begin and develop his relationship with God the Father through Jesus Christ (Matthew 28:18-20, Matthew 19: 13-15).

CLASSICAL

In all its levels, programs, and teaching, Logos School seeks to:
   A. Emphasize grammar, logic, and rhetoric in all subjects (see definitions below);
   B. Encourage every student to develop a love for learning and live up to his academic potential;
   C. Provide an orderly atmosphere conducive to the attainment of the above goals.

   Definitions:
   Grammar—The fundamental rules of each subject.
   Logic—The ordered relationship of particulars in each subject.

Rhetoric—How the grammar and logic of each subject may be clearly expressed.

THE LATIN PROGRAM

The Latin program at Logos is designed to be in step with the characteristics of the ages taught and so enable Latin to be learned well and enjoyed.

Latin instruction begins in the third grade. Two characteristics of this age make it a suitable time to begin. Students have mastered the basic vocabulary and grammar of English in reading, writing, speaking, and listening; and they enjoy memory work. This enjoyment is used in vocabulary acquisition and in the entrenchment of paradigms which will make the Latin work in the years ahead more pleasant rather than intolerably difficult.

Most of the vocabulary is concrete—*taurus, aquila*, and *navis* are easier to lodge in a third grade mind than *ab, sed* and *prope*. Their knowledge of their native tongue can be used profitably to instruct them in Latin grammar. If you say to a group of children, "You am smart," you will be greeted by hoots of laughter. That grasp of English makes *sum, es, est* understandable and at the same time illumines the language that they gained naturally. The work of the second year reinforces and adds to the vocabulary and paradigms learned in the first year. The grammar work becomes more involved. To translate *audebo* as "I will dare" was easy enough for the previous year. The analysis required to translate "I will dare" into Latin is more suitable for this age. Also there are opportunities for English grammar to be corrected by the Latin work. Improper grammar is not the only kind ever subjected to laughter. The first time a Latin class is told that it is proper to say "It is I" rather than "It is me," skepticism is likely to abound.

In the third and fourth years, complexity increases as does abstraction, analysis, and the necessity of attending to detail. The rewards of Latin at this level are the rewards of greater maturity and "real Latin" can be sampled to a greater degree than the mottoes and short quotations of the earlier years.

First Year Latin
Third Grade

GOALS
1. Correct pronunciation of Latin letters and words.
2. Vocabulary of 450 Latin words.

3. Recognition of Latin derivatives in English, use of dictionary for etymology, growth in English vocabulary.
4. Understanding and use of grammar in Latin and English.
   Latin: Declension of first and second declension nouns. Conjugation of first and second conjugation verbs.
   English and Latin: concepts of singular and plural; present, past, and future tense; nouns, verbs, and adjectives; first, second, and third persons; word order.
5. Memorization of beginning Latin paradigms in chants.
6. Exposure to Latin quotes and expressions.
7. Simple translation work.
8. Some knowledge of Roman history.
   The Latin classes are held Monday, Wednesday, and Friday for forty-five minutes. A quiz is given each Friday, mainly over the fifteen vocabulary words for that week. Every seventh week will be a review week, and a cumulative test will be given on that Friday.

Sample Vocabulary Lists
Third Grade—Week 19

1. lupus,-i	wolf	
2. nimbus,-i	cloud or storm	
3. taurus,-i	bull	
4. aura,-ae	breeze	
5. herba,-ae	herb, plant	
6. spelunca,-ae	cave	
7. aquila,-ae	eagle	
8. ripa,-ae	bank, shore	
9. floreo	I flourish	
10. exploro	I find out	
11. occulto	I hide	
12. delecto	I delight	
13. clam	secretly	
14. bene	well	
15. satis	enough	
	i	imus
	isti	istis
	it	erunt

Fourth Grade

1. laetus, a, um — happy
2. antiquus, a, um — ancient
3. mirus, a, um — strange, wonderful
4. fabula,-ae — story
5. avus,-i — grandfather
6. mater, matris — mother
7. pater, patris — father
8. frater, fratris — brother
9. soror, sororis — sister
10. iter, itineris — journey
11. designo, are — mark out
12. considero, are — contemplate
13. habito, habitare — inhabit, live in
14. commemoro, commemorare — call to mind
15. recito, recitare — read aloud

Review Test
Third Grade

I. Translate these words.

1. verbum _____
2. folium _____
3. satis _____
4. spelunca _____
5. signum _____
6. populus _____
7. clamo _____
8. regina _____
9. stagnum _____
10. beneficium _____
11. potens _____
12. corona _____
13. auxilium _____
14. urbs _____
15. nego _____
16. lupus _____
17. taurus _____
18. aedificium _____
19. civis _____
20. miser _____
21. murus _____
22. pugna _____
23. ferus _____
24. hostis _____
25. nuntius _____

II. Write singular or plural in the first blank, and translate in the second blank.

1. sagittae _____   _____
2. iniuria _____   _____
3. praefectus _____   _____
4. captivi _____   _____

III. Translate these.

1. manent _____
2. putamus _____
3. perturbas_____
4. nocet _____
5. augeo_____
6. prohibes _____

IV. Translate these sentences.

1. Aquilae occultant_____
2. Aura delectat _____
3. Socius iuvat_____

Test

Given to all classes (grades three—six) at beginning of the term

Use these Latin words and your sharp brain to match these English words to their definitions.

corpus	body
nihil	nothing
terra	land, earth
doceo	I teach
bellum	war
avis	bird
Deus	God
flumen	river
laudo	I praise
novus	new
animus	mind
mare	sea
vivo	I live
voco	I call
sol	sun
magnus	big, great

1. terrestrial	9. flume
2. marine	10. Deity
3. solstice	11. corpse
4. nihilist	12. novelty
5. magnanimous	13. vivacity
6. belligerent	14. vociferate
7. docile	15. vocation
8. aviary	16. laudable

a) Two times during the year when the sun has no apparent
   northward or southward movement_____
b) worthy of praise_____
c) an artificial channel for a stream of
   water_____
d) a person who believes nothing is worth believing
   in_____
e) a large enclosure for birds_____
f) God_____
g) having to do with the earth or its inhabi-
   tants_____
h) liveliness_____
i) having to do with the sea or its inhabi-
   tants_____
j) to cry out loudly_____
k) teachable_____
l) warlike_____
m) a dead body_____
n) a calling_____
o) great in mind and heart_____
p) something that is new_____

Martha Sebring, instructor of Latin, Logos School

NINTH GRADE HISTORY CLASS

Studies in General History
Reformation and Renaissance Era

   3. Extracts Illustrative of Life and Thought of the Time
   a. From Letters of Columbus to the Spanish Chancellor of
      the Exchequer and to the Spanish Monarchs, "respecting
      the Islands found in the Indies." (Hakluyt Society.)
         "Believing that you will take pleasure in hearing of the
      great success which our Lord has granted me in my voy-
      age, I write you this letter, whereby you will learn how in
      thirty-three days' time I reached the Indies with the fleet
      which the most illustrious king and queen, our sovereigns,
      gave to me, where I found very many islands thickly peo-
      pled, of all which I took possession . . . for their

Highnesses. . . . San Domingo is a wonder, its mountains and plains, and meadows, and fields are so beautiful and rich for planting and sowing, and rearing cattle of all kinds, and for building towns and villages. The harbors on the coast, and the number and size and wholesomeness of the rivers, most of them bearing gold, surpass anything that would be believed. . . . Our Redeemer hath granted this victory to our illustrious king and queen, . . . who have acquired great fame by an event of such high importance, in which all Christendom ought to rejoice, and which it ought to celebrate with great festivals and the offering of solemn thanks to the Holy Trinity, . . . both for the great exaltation which may accrue to them in turning so many nations to our holy faith, and also for the temporal benefits which will bring great refreshment and gain, not only to Spain, but to all Christians."

". . . In all the countries visited by your Highnesses' ships, I have caused a high cross to be fixed upon every headland, and have proclaimed to every nation that I have discovered, the lofty estate of your Highnesses and of your court in Spain. I also tell them all I can respecting our holy faith and of the belief in the holy Mother Church. . . . Your Highnesses have become the masters of another world, where our holy faith may become so much increased, and whence such stores of wealth may be derived."

b. From Sir Walter Raleigh's Account of the Discovery of Guiana (Hakluyt Society.)

" . . . The common soldier shal here fight for gold, and pay himselfe in steede of pence, with plates of halfe a foote brode, whereas he breaketh his bones in other warres for . . . penury. Those commanders and Chieftaines, that shoote at honour and abundance, shal find there more rich and bewtifull cities, more temples adorned with golden Images, more sepulchers filled with treasure, than . . . Cortes found in Mexico . . . and the shining glorie of this conquest will eclipse all those so farre extended beames of the Spanish nation. . . .The soile besides is so excellent and so full of rivers, as it will carrie sugar, ginger, and all those other commodities which the West Indies hath. . . . For whatsoever Prince shall possesse it, shall bee greatest, and if the king of Spayne enjoy it, he will become unrresistable. . . . I trust in God . . . that he which is . . .

Lorde of Lords, will put it into her hart which is Lady of
Ladies to possesse it."
d. From Letters of Luther to Pope Leo X (about 1518).
"I have heard the worst account, most blessed father,
touching myself, namely, that certain friends have made
my name most odious to you and yours, as of one who
was labouring to diminish the authority and power of the
keys and of the Supreme Pontiff; and that I am called a
heretic, an apostate, a traitor, and a thousand other igno-
minious names. These things shock and amaze me; one
thing only sustains me, a sense of innocence."
He goes on to speak thus of his theses: "By what unlucky
chance it is, that these particular propositions of mine, more than
all others, should go forth into nearly all the earth, I am at a loss to
know. They were set forth here for our use alone, and how they
should come to everybody's knowledge is incredible to me. . . . But
what shall I do? Recall them I cannot; and yet I see that their noto-
riety bringeth upon me great odium. In order, then, to soften my
adversaries and to gratify many friends, I send forth these trifles
(proofs, etc.) to explain my theses. For the greater safety I let them
go forth, most blessed father, under your name, and under the
shadow of your protection. Here, all who will may see how sincerely
I honor the ecclesiastical power and reverence the Keys, and also
how basely I am reproached and belied by my enemies. . . . Save or
slay, call or recall, approve or disapprove, as it shall best please you.
I will acknowledge your voice as the voice of Christ presiding and
speaking in you."
To his friend Spalatin he writes: "A heretic I will never be; err
I may in disputation. But I wish to decide no doctrine; only I am not
willing to be the slave of the opinions of men."
To Staupitz, "I see that attempts are made at Rome that the
kingdom of truth, i.e., of Christ, be no longer the kingdom of
truth. . . . But I desire to belong to this kingdom. . . . I learn from
experience that the people are sighing for the voice of their
Shepherd, Christ, and the youth are burning with wonderful zeal for
the sacred oracles. A beginning is made with us in reading of Greek.
We are all giving ourselves to the Greek for the better understanding of the Bible. We are expecting a Hebrew teacher, and the elector
hath the business in hand."
On seeing the first brief which condemned him, he exclaims:

Reprinted from *Studies in General History* by Mary S. Barnes, first female faculty member of Stanford
University. The book is published by Norwood Press, J. S. Cushing and Co., Berwich and Smith,
Boston, MA, February 11, 1896.

"It is incredible that a thing so monstrous should come from the chief pontiff, especially from Leo X. . . . If, in truth, it did come forth from the Roman court, then I will show them their most licentious temerity and their most ungodly ignorance."

STUDY ON 3

1. What are the two prominent objects of exploration and conquest in the mind of Columbus?
2. Name three qualities of character displayed by his letters.
3. What motives for exploration are shown by Sir Walter Raleigh?
4. What national rivalry?
5. Taking a and b as typical, what classes of men will be drawn to the new countries?
6. What is the attitude of Luther toward the Church?
7. Toward what he believes to be the truth?
8. What do these extracts show of his character?
9. What reason do they show for the attitude of the reformers toward Greek scholarship?

PHONICS—GRADE ONE

Sample first grade phonics lessons taken from:
The Sing, Spell, Read, and Write Program
Beginning of the Year

1. Review letter sounds.
2. Teach Phonics Song A to Z (every day and point to pictures as we sing). "A, A, apple; B, B, ball; C, C, cat; and D, D, doll, etc." (Refer to ditto Step 1.)
3. Teach phonics games to reinforce: *Pick-a-Sound . . . a "Go Fish" sort of card game where students ask for letter sounds to make pairs. *Sound-O . . . Just like Bingo, but using letters and letter sounds. *When a child masters a step, sign it, and move on.
4. By Step 3 on ditto, they learn the Short Vowel Song and Point-Along.
5. At Step 4 on ditto, they cut out Ferris wheel tickets and learn to sing and ride the Ferris wheel. (There is a big one in class as well.) They put letter sounds together that will eventually form words. For instance, a trip around the Ferris wheel with ticket "g" would go: "ga-", "ge-", "gi-", "go-", "gu-",

"go-", "gi-", "ge-", "ga-." We talk about some of the words they know that start like that and see if they can already spell some of them, such as: *get, God, gum.*

6. We use only short vowel sounds to avoid confusion. The words are: "Round and round and up and down the Ferris wheel we go. Round and round and up and down, come on now don't be slow. Have your ticket in your hand; the ride will soon begin. Do your best, your very best, go round and round again!"

   We sing the chorus between each set of tickets (star, square, circle, triangle, bell, house, and flag). As each child can do it without help, sign the shape and move on.

Middle to End of the Year

1. Letter Cluster Phonics Song (same tune as Phonics A to Z Song). It takes two to three weeks to learn all the clusters in the song.
2. Pick-a-Sound Game (same as Pick-a-Sound Card game with A to Z except using letter clusters in this deck).
3. "Pop" the Balloons—reinforces letter clusters and tests each child. The child may color the balloons of the clusters he or she knows.
4. Duck Pond—reinforces again and tests. Children cut out little letter cluster ducks and may take them off their ponds if they know the cluster. This letter cluster learning takes a number of weeks depending on the students (three to six weeks).
5. Reading books accompany nearly all the steps on the raceway. They reinforce what is being taught at each step using fun-to-read stories.
6. Spelling lists begin at Step 5 (see ditto) and reinforce the sounds and clusters as well.
7. Reading vocabulary and comprehension tests are given through the first fourteen steps in the book.

By the end of the year, if a group is particularly fast, they will reach Step 36 (refer to ditto). They will be able to read, write, and spell these words! Step 21 is the goal for the first grade.

SAMPLE EXCERPTS FROM LOGOS SCHOOL CURRICULUM PRINCIPLES

Elementary

1. Bible—We seek to:
   a) Have the students read the actual text themselves.
   b) Teach the Biblical pattern of salvation—law before grace.
2. English—We seek to:
   a) Put a major emphasis on good writing by requiring the students to write often and correctly in every area of learning.
   b) Introduce the students to many styles of writing using the Bible and other high-quality literature.
3. Social Studies—We seek to:
   a) Teach the students that God is in control of history, and He will determine its ultimate goal.
   b) Enable the students to see God's hand in the history of the world and the United States.
4. Science—We seek to:
   a) Teach that the Biblical creation account is true, and the theory of evolution is false.
   b) Show the students that because God made the universe, it has order that makes it possible to hypothesize and experiment.
5. Mathematics—We seek to:
   a) Put an emphasis on conceptual as well as specific understanding through the frequent use of story problems.
   b) Illustrate God's unchanging attributes through the logical and mathematical system He gave to mankind.
6. Reading—We seek to:
   a) Use phonics as the primary tool for beginning reading.
   b) Introduce the students to high-quality children's literature as soon as possible through our Literature program.
7. Art—We seek to:
   a) Encourage the students to appreciate and imitate the beauty of the creation in many art forms.
   b) Introduce the students to the masters' works of Western culture (primarily, not exclusively).
8. Music—We seek to:
   a) Train the students to sing knowledgeably and joyfully to the Lord on a regular basis.
   b) Enrich the teaching of Scripture through the teaching of numerous, high-quality hymns.

9. Physical Education—We seek to:
a) Encourage the students to knowledgeably establish and maintain good health and nutritional habits.
b) Enhance Biblical patterns of behavior through cooperation, teamwork, and good sportsmanship.

Secondary

1. Bible—We seek to:
a) Encourage contextual understanding of basic Christian doctrine and principles.
b) Provide practical opportunities for students to demonstrate Christ's love through community service and in-school projects.
2. English—We seek to:
a) Introduce the students to a wide assortment of outstanding authors, books, poetry, plays, etc., of appropriate level.
b) Give the students an appreciation for the literary style and makeup of the Bible in order to aid comprehension.
3. Social Studies—We seek to:
a) Familiarize the students with primary sources and critical historical documents.
b) Help the students understand what their cultural heritage is and how all areas of knowledge interrelate in the making of history. Make history, government, and economics "three-dimensional" to the students through a multitude of teaching methods and materials, e.g., photos, music, art, architecture, food, speakers, etc.
4. Science—We seek to:
a) Show that scientific investigation is only possible in a God-designed, orderly universe.
b) Give the students an appreciation for the magnificence, complexity, and immensity of the creation.
5. Mathematics—We seek to:
a) Ensure that the students have a thorough mastery of basic mathematic functions, formulas, and tables.
b) Instill an enjoyment of math in all students.

6. Physical Education—We seek to:
  a) Encourage Biblical patterns of behavior in team and individual sports by emphasizing cooperation, teamwork, good sportsmanship, and hard work.
  b) Give the students an appreciation for and an introduction to the skills and rules necessary to perform many popular team/individual sports.

STATEMENT OF FAITH

The following is the foundation of beliefs on which Logos School is based. They are also the key elements of Christianity that will be taught in various ways through all the grade levels. The substance of these statements will be considered primary doctrine in Logos. Secondary or any divisive issues will not be presented as primary doctrine.

1. We believe the Bible to be the only inerrant, authoritative Word of God.
2. We believe that there is one God, eternally existent in three Persons: Father, Son, and Holy Spirit.
3. We believe in the deity of our Lord Jesus Christ, in His virgin birth, in His sinless life, in His miracles, in His vicarious and atoning death through His shed blood, in His bodily resurrection, in His ascension to the right hand of the Father, and in His personal return in power and glory.
4. We believe that for the salvation of lost and sinful men, regeneration by the Holy Spirit is absolutely necessary.
5. We believe that salvation is by grace through faith alone.
6. We believe that faith without works is dead.
7. We believe in the present ministry of the Holy Spirit by whose indwelling the Christian is enabled to live a godly life.
8. We believe in the resurrection of both the saved and the lost: they that are saved to the resurrection of life and they that are lost to the resurrection of damnation.
9. We believe in the spiritual unity of all believers in our Lord Jesus Christ.

TABLE B-1			

GRAMMATICAL TABLE

SUBJECT	THIRD GRADE	FOURTH GRADE	FIFTH GRADE
Math	Addition, subtraction, and multiplication facts	Division facts	Division facts, decimal chart
Bible	Bible verses	Bible verses, and books of the Bible	Review books of Bible, memorize more verses
Reading	NA	NA	NA
English	Spelling rules	Spelling rules/lists	Spelling/occasional rules
History Geography	U. S. states, capitals, and major cities	Dates, names, U. S. presidents	Countries, capitals, rivers, geographic features
Science	Recent curriculum change	Recent curriculum change	Recent curriculum change
Latin	Vocabulary, case-endings, conjugations	Continue work on case-endings, conjugations	New curriculum development in progress

Note: It must be remembered that this is a table of some of the "grammar" memorized. It is *not* a table of course objectives or of how much material is covered in each subject. Also, review is normally necessary; it is imperative when we have students coming to us in the fourth grade who were not at Logos for the third grade. What is review for their classmates is frequently new to them.

A BRIEF HISTORICAL SKETCH

*I*t may helpful for Christians to understand how we got to this point historically and why a book such as this was necessary. Christians are too often reactionary. If there is a particular problem at the local public school, parents react to it. This does not necessarily mean they have a good understanding of the ideological war that has been with us for over a hundred years.

Before sketching an outline of the history of public education, it is important to emphasize that it is a sketch. When dealing with movements like the public school movement, it is too easy for Christians to be reactionary and say that the cause of A was B, and nothing but B. But as any student of history should know, life is not that simple. Nevertheless, it *is* possible to identify, in a broad way, how we got into our current situation; consequently, I assume below that B had a lot to do with it.

The establishment of public education in America can be described as a dedicated effort from the very beginning to live by bread alone. Jesus referred to Deuteronomy 8:3, which says that "man does not live on bread alone but on every word that comes from the mouth of the Lord." Those who established public education sought to build a school system without reference to the Word of God. [1]

History is full of utopian philosophers and thinkers. We have always had them. *Utopia* is a word that comes to us from the Greek and literally means "no place." Dreamers have always loved to fashion these hypothetical realms. When such thinkers described their utopias, they were describing what they thought the ideal society would be. When Plato (428-348 B.C.) wrote his *Republic*, he wrote out a set of suggested laws—what he would do, what he would ban, what he would establish, and so on.[2]

Millennia later, Marx did the same thing. But because of the rebellion against Christianity, introduced in the Renaissance and continued in the Enlightenment, the climate was right for followers of Marx to try to put utopian ideas into practice. One of the things that distinguishes Plato from Marx is that Marx had the misfortune of having someone actually try what he advocated. If Plato's Republic were actually built, that society would most certainly be a totalitarian hellhole. It would be a hideous place to live, but that doesn't tarnish Plato's reputation at all. This is because his utopia stayed a utopia, which is to say, "no place." But Marx was not just a dreamer; he wanted to change history.[3] The political climate was right for attempts to build the City of Man.[4]

Enter public schools. One of the interesting features of the Communist Manifesto was the demand for free public education. In the words of Marx and Engels:

> But, you will say, we destroy the most hallowed of relations when we replace home education by social.
>
> And your education! Is not that also social, and determined by the social conditions under which you educate, by the intervention of society, direct or indirect, by means of schools, etc.? The Communists have not invented the intervention of society in education; they do but seek to alter the character of that intervention and to rescue education from the influence of the ruling class.[5]

Notice here the communist demand that education be understood as a social function, rather than a familial function. This was not a new idea. The concept that children belong to the state goes back at least to Plato. Marx and Engels thought that education was socialized already, but that the ideals imparted to the children were all wrong. Communist "socialized" education was ideologically pure and had the additional advantage of honesty. At least the communists admitted what they were trying to do. A little later, when they got to their list of demands, we find that the first part of the tenth demand insists upon free education "for all children in public schools."[6]

The founders of public education in America were not communists, but they certainly had imbibed the spirit of their age.[7] That spirit was statist, i.e., it looked to the state for answers. In that sense, the founders of public education in America and the communists had a common faith, and that faith was in state-controlled education.

We often have quaint prejudices about the nineteenth century. Our images sometimes have little to do with the way things actually were. It is the nature of such prejudices to equip us to believe, not only falsehoods, but bizarre falsehoods. For example, when I was in the navy submarine service, I had the opportunity to visit Cuba. We pulled into Guantanamo Bay, and when I came up out of the hatch and looked at Cuba for the first time, I was shocked. Why? It was in color. Up to that time, my image of communist countries had been in black and white. They looked like a newsprint photo of some cold East European place—in the rain. That was communism, and the sight of totalitarianism in technicolor threw me.

We have the same problem with many of our notions about the nineteenth century. We think it was a time of great traditional piety, morality, and so forth. In some quarters this was true; the Christians were godly and upright. But it was also a time of incredible revolutionary ferment. Our civilization was beginning to unravel. Some people were going in all directions, trying out all sorts of new social experiments. We tend to think of communism as a twentieth-century rather than a nineteenth-century phenomenon. But the nineteenth century was the time when communism was in the full vigor of youth. The latter part of the twentieth century, however, has been the time of communism's dotage.[8]

In the same way, we tend to think of radical socialism in education as something developed in the late 1960s by a modern NEA. Only since that time has it corrupted our public school system. But radicalism in education began at the very start of public education in America. *It was the driving intellectual force for the public school movement.*

This does not mean there never had been a Christian "public" school system. They were rare, and they were unlike the public schools of today, but they did exist. They were recognizably public schools in that they were tax-supported, or supported out of the public treasury. Luther had advocated public education in Germany at the time of the Reformation, and John Knox had done the same in Scotland in the Scottish Reformation.[9] Closer to home, the New England Puritans supported a form of public education.[10] The key thing to remember is that these Christians did not have to worry about the problem of pluralism in education at all. For example, the Scotland of John Knox was Calvinistic, and after the Catholics had been driven out of power, the country was overwhelmingly

Reformed.[11] Consequently, there was no problem about what faith to teach in the "public" schools. Luther faced the same basic situation.

In New England, the schools were not public schools in the modern sense of the term. They were religious schools, supported by a state that was also religious. This is not to say that this system was a good idea. I contend that God did not give the responsibility for education to the government, even if the officials are godly. However, my point is that the problems then were different in kind from the problems of the modern public school.

It is also important to remember that what is obvious in the fruit is not always obvious in the bud. Many of the Christians who advocated this state-supported education did not know what sort of fruit would come from it. The New England Puritans envisioned a godly education fitting into an all-encompassing godly society. They didn't know that the tool they created would be captured and used by the opposition—which leads to the next point.

When the United States was born, the only public school in America was in Boston. As already mentioned, it was not really a public school. Children had to be literate to be admitted; they had already been taught to read in private schools. Once the child knew how to read and was seven years old, he could enter the school system.

At this time, a Scottish socialist named Robert Owen was promulgating his ideas about the perfectibility of man.[12] He believed that man is by nature basically good. He does evil only because of the way he is taught. Society's job, therefore, is to reach children at a very early age and teach them to be good. Owen thought it necessary for progressive thinkers like himself to take control of education, and the sooner the better. American utopians took up his ideas.

In 1819, when Prussia adopted a very regimented public school system, the American utopian activists had a model. (Robert Owen contended that the Prussians got the idea from him.) Horace Mann, one of these activists, became the secretary of the Massachusetts Board of Education in 1837. He was able to make use of the "public" schools created earlier by the Puritans. Mann, however, had a different agenda. He wrote:

> Let the Common School be expanded to its capabilities, let it be worked with the efficiency of which it is susceptible, and nine-tenths of the crimes in the penal code would become obsolete; the long catalogue of human ills would be abridged; men would

walk more safely by day; every pillow would be more inviolable by night; property, life, and character held by a stronger tenure; all rational hopes respecting the future brightened.[13]

Nine-tenths of the crimes in the penal code would become obsolete? This man, the father of public education in America, really believed that the state, by means of the school, could be our savior. The public schools have been steadily laboring at the work of our culture's salvation ever since. So radicalism was planted in the public school movement from the very beginning; there were great messianic expectations. They said we will transform society, eliminate sin, eradicate crime, and deal with vice. Isn't it is cheaper to build schools than prisons?

These schools were not permissive. There was discipline and hard work, and as far as "the basics" were concerned, a good education was provided. But this did not change the radical agenda at the heart of the public school system. It illustrates for us a real problem with Christians fighting for control of the public schools. What many want to do is push the public schools back to what they were in the 1950s. If they were able to reestablish the public schools of an Ozzie and Harriet era, they would be happy. And if they succeeded in getting back the public schools of the 1880s, they would be deliriously happy. In short, if the public schools were not so visibly corrupt, it would not be difficult for many Christians to return to them.

But many Christians do not understand the underlying clash of principles. The radicals of the last century were not lax disciplinarians; they gave the children a rigorous education. But it was apart from the applied Word of God. *It was bread alone.* And as history teaches us, when man attempts to live by bread alone, it is simply a matter of time before he has no bread. Discipline, classics, tradition, punctuality, and hard work do not make a godly education. It is possible to have all these things, and have nothing more than a public school of ninety to a hundred years ago. If someone were watching a movie on videotape and didn't like how it was turning out, he wouldn't rewind it and try it again. But many Christians are saying they don't like the way the public schools are going, and they try to rewind the system back to the 1950s or to the turn of the century. They do not realize that the radicalism bearing fruit now was planted in the last century, and the seed was anti-Christian.

Of course, those who ran the schools at the local level were not all radicals. The schools were considered to be bastions of Protestant Christianity, but only because there was still a great deal of local control over the schools. Because the general populace was Protestant, so were the schools. The Catholics began their parochial school system in response. But the intellectual leaders of the movement to establish public schools were not friends to Biblical Christianity.

We must also remember the difference between many of the western states, which are essentially provinces, and the eastern states. The original thirteen colonies were established long before the United States came into being. They began their existence under the rule of England, and after the war for independence, they each became independent and sovereign states. Those thirteen states came together in Congress and created the federal Constitution. The federal government is younger than these thirteen states and is their child.

But once the nation expanded westward, the central government began to create new states. The roles of the central government and state governments were now reversed. It is arguable that most of the western states developed a provincial mentality; i.e., they were creations of the federal government and considered themselves beholden to it.

Here is another reversal of expectations. When we think of the West in the last century, we like to think of the Sacketts, John Wayne, a Winchester over the fireplace, and a red-checked tablecloth. We most certainly do not think of radicalism, communism, and socialism. But it was to the western states that educational statists moved, establishing public education from the very beginning. In the East are private schools that are older than the United States. But in the western states, the public schools, as they exist today, were the first schools established.

Consequently, competition between the private sector and the public sector in the West is much less. Clashes between private educators and the state illustrate this lack of competition. A few years ago a pastor in Nebraska was thrown in jail for not having an accredited school. Nebraska? Not Massachusetts? Again we see that this conflict did not begin in the 1960s. Earlier in this century, it was against the law in Nebraska to teach a child a language other than English.[14] The state presumed it had the authority over such things. The measure was struck down as unconstitutional by the Supreme Court. A law in Oregon around the same time completely forbade private education.[15] That law was also struck down as unconstitutional.

Education in the western provinces was in the control of humanistic thinkers who established what they wanted from the ground up. So when we began building a private school in Idaho, we were part of a historically significant movement. Building a private school in the East may evoke a sense of returning to one's roots. In the West, Christian educators are planting something new.

As we look at the state of public education today, we can see that the promise has not been fulfilled. The messianic fervor that accompanied the early advocates of public education is also gone, and we are in the privileged position of being able to see the collapse of a false savior. Fifty years ago, the points made in a book such as this would not have found a sympathetic hearing—even in the Christian community. Back then public schools had dress codes; the kids weren't listening to their Walkmans during class; and rape, murder, and drug-dealing weren't the problems they are today.

But all the deterioration we see today came from somewhere. It grew out of the public schools of thirty, forty, fifty, and a hundred years ago, and we are privileged to witness the breakdown of another god that failed. It is important to remember that the messianic expectations did not begin ten years ago, but more than a hundred years ago. The devotees of this ideal have worked for over a century to implement the agenda. It still isn't working. Like all attempted utopias, the reality falls far short of expectations.[16]

NOTES

CHAPTER ONE: *The Education Crisis*

1. My two companions were Larry Lucas and Shirley Quist. The school is greatly in debt to both of them.
2. It was disconcerting to me to read a recent editorial in *Christianity Today* that seeks to honor parents "who have not retreated from the public schools." *Christianity Today*, September 22, 1989, p. 14.
3. The extent of our involvement was not planned; it just happened. As I write this, I am teaching civics and Bible in our secondary program, and my wife is teaching English and American literature.
4. In other words, there is a shortage of information in the minds of students. There is no shortage of information about the first shortage. We are awash in studies that demonstrate the crisis in education.
5. *A Nation at Risk*, National Commission on Excellence in Education, (Washington, DC: U. S. Government Printing Office, 1983), p. 8.
6. "Reforming Math Education," *Science News*, February 4, 1989, p. 70. But astonishingly, one key proposal of the report calls for a change from pencil/paper exercises and rote memorization! Maybe computers and calculators can save us.
7. I. Peterson, "Education: Math and Aftermath," *Science News*, January 31, 1987, p. 72.
8. The fact that Canadians did well indicates that we have a problem with our *schools*. If our decline were attributable to a general cultural malaise, the chances are good that Canadians would share in it.
9. *Physics Today*, April 1989, p. 45. They are citing a report called *A World of Difference*. Also mentioned was a report by the National Research Council entitled *Everybody Counts*, which indicated that everybody doesn't.
10. B. F. Sommerville, "What's Wrong with Science Education in America?" *Chemical Engineering Progress*, December 1989, p. 70. The same article referred to another study where the United States came in third from the last, ahead of Hong Kong and the Philippines.

11. *See also* the essay by Charles Krauthammer, "Education: Doing Bad and Feeling Good," in *Time*, February 5, 1990. And in this regard, it is worthwhile to remember a line out of *The Gondoliers*, an operetta by Gilbert and Sullivan. "When everyone is somebody, then no one's anybody!"

12. Timothy Beardsley, "Case Proved," *Scientific American*, May 1989, p. 22.

13. Mortimer Zuckerman, "The Lost Generation," *U. S. News and World Report*, August 21, 1989, p. 68.

14. Sommerville, "What's Wrong," *Chemical Engineering Progress*, p. 72. This was a 1985/86 survey.

15. *U.S. News and World Report*, January 2, 1989, p. 97.

16. One of our Logos students made it to our state's finals in that geography bee. It would be an interesting study for someone to investigate the percentages of privately schooled students in such national competitions.

17. All in all, it appears the education establishment has taken the advice offered by Pink Floyd: "Hey, teacher! Leave them kids alone!"

18. *A Nation at Risk*, p. 21.

19. Nancy Perry, "Saving the Schools: How Business Can Help," *Fortune*, November 7, 1988, p. 43.

20. Dan Goodgame, "Calling for an Overhaul," *Time*, October 9, 1989, p. 69. For example, former Secretary of Education William Bennett dismissed much of what he heard at the summit as "pap—and stuff that rhymes with pap."

21. For example, a glance at some of the suggested solutions in the summit transcripts reveals the extent of our problem. Consider the following from former Secretary of Education Cavazos. "And the main point that I saw and heard the discussion was—major role in terms of the Department of Education—the U. S. Department of Education and how it relates to the rest of the nation. Clearly asking for leadership, for assessment, what works." Press briefing by Secretary of Education Cavazos, September 27, 1989, The White House, Office of the Press Secretary.

22. After all, if Japanese students today are running circles around us, then it is unreasonable to accuse reformers of setting unrealistic standards that they claim were met in some fictional past. If the standards are unrealistic, then why can these other countries meet them?

23. Morton Kondrake, "Sorry Summit," *The New Republic*, October 23, 1989, p. 14.

24. Nyberg and Egan, *The Erosion of Education* (New York: Teachers College Press, 1981), p. 6.

25. *Ibid.*, pp. 5, 7, 10.

26. Peter McLaren, *Life in Schools* (New York: Longman, 1989), pp. 15, 20. Incidentally, McLaren includes conservative Christians in his list of horrors facing our society.

27. For example, "There is little evidence that schools are less successful in carrying out their tasks of transmitting basic skills, for instance, than formerly, but we now have higher expectations of what schools can and should do." Jeanne Ballantine, *The Sociology of Education* (Englewood Cliffs, NJ: Prentice-Hall, 1983), p. 52.

28. Ralph Tyler, "Societal Expectations for the American School: A Long View," in *Education in the 80s: Curricular Challenges* (Washington, DC: National Education Association, 1981), p. 16.

29. *Ibid.*, p. 15.
30. Michael Apple, *Teachers and Texts* (New York: Routledge and Kegan Paul, 1986), p. 128. "Report after report, with *A Nation at Risk* being the best-known and most powerful, has pointed a finger at 'our failing schools.' In many ways, this still seems odd." Notice the quotation marks around 'our failing schools.'
31. Even though published in the 1970s, a clear example of this kind of truculence is Postman and Weingartner, *The School Book* (New York: Dell Publishing, 1973), pp. 82-93. The chapter is an incredible collection of *non sequiturs*, including the observation that Herr Goebbels, minister of propaganda for the Third Reich, knew how to read.
32. David Harman, *Illiteracy: A National Dilemma* (New York: Cambridge, 1987), p. 47.
33. At least in the movie, one of Clark's main methods of problem-solving appears to have been yelling.
34. *Newsweek*, July 4, 1988, p. 60. There is, however, some indication of coming change in Chicago. In 1989, the Board of Education was replaced with a parent-led board for each public school.
35. *Nation at Risk*, p. 8.
36. Connie Leslie, "In Search of Excellence," *Newsweek*, October 24, 1988, p. 81.
37. Thomas Sowell, *Education: Assumptions Versus History* (Stanford, CA: Hoover Institution Press, 1986), p. 103.
38. Linwood Laughy, *The Interactive Parent* (Kooskia, ID: Mountain Meadow Press, 1988), p. 12.
39. Susan Ohanian, "Yes, but Where Are Your Credits in Recess Management 101?" *The Washington Monthly*, April 1984, p. 40.
40. See, for example, the *Wall Street Journal*, November 2, 1989, A1 and A14. There are two stories of interest. The headline of one is: "Classroom Scandal/Cheaters in Schools May Not Be Students, but Their Teachers." The other noted that the questions on tests are often matched in kits and study booklets.
41. "Helping Students Cheat," AP report, *The Idahonian/Daily News*, September 9, 1989.
42. Myron Lieberman, *Beyond Public Education* (New York: Praeger Publishers, 1986), p. 11.
43. This problem is the result of hysteria concerning population growth. But the population bomb never did explode, and our work force is diminishing.
44. Joan Ratteray, "Suppressing Innovation; The Corporate Role in Education," *Vital Speeches of the Day*, February 1, 1988, p. 246.
45. Jerry Hume, "Business Must Stop Supporting Failure," *Point of View Paper* (Washington, DC: The Heritage Foundation, 1989), p. 3.
46. Allan Bloom, *The Closing of the American Mind* (New York: Simon and Schuster, 1987), p. 62.
47. Robert Pattison, *On Literacy* (Oxford: Oxford University Press, 1982), p. 200.
48. L. Butterfield, ed., *Diary and Autobiography of John Adams* (Cambridge, MA: Harvard University Press, 1961).
49. Dupont de Nemours, *National Education in the United States of America*,

(Newark, DE: University of Delaware Press, 1923), p. 3. The report goes on, " . . . while in Spain, Portugal, Italy, only a sixth of the population can read; in Germany, even in France, not more than a third; in Poland, about two men in a hundred; and in Russia not one in two hundred." It should be noted, however, that the figures for the United States did not include the slave population. This study is cited by Rousas Rushdoony, *The Messianic Character of American Education* (Nutley, NJ: Craig Press, 1979), pp. 329-330.

50. Myron Tuman, *A Preface to Literacy* (Tuscaloosa, AL: The University of Alabama Press, 1987), p. 34.

51. The last national survey was done twelve years ago, but at that time, one in twenty teachers had been attacked on the job. In 1987, nearly 184,000 people "were injured as a result of school crime in one year." The figure includes staff, students, and visitors. *Teacher Magazine*, May 1990, p. 58.

CHAPTER TWO: *Suggested Secular and Christian Reforms*

1. Even though there is consensus that "a problem" exists, differences in the worldview of various reformers nevertheless will affect the standards by which the reformers measure the schools.

2. *A Nation at Risk*, National Commission on Excellence in Education, (Washington, DC: U. S. Government Printing Office, 1983), p. 3.

3. There is one structural reform that I will not develop, for obvious reasons. It is the reform suggested by H. L. Mencken, when he observed there was nothing wrong with education that could not be solved by burning all the schools and hanging all the teachers.

4. *A Nation at Risk*, p. 33.

5. Michael Kirst, "Adequate Financial Support for Education Is Essential," *Today's Education (NEA Today)*, 1985-86, p. 22.

6. *Digest of Education Statistics*, 1987, pp. 94, 112.

7. At Logos it costs us around $180 a month to educate a child. Tuition covers only a portion of this; the rest must come from outside support. Compare this figure to the $437 a month it costs to educate a child in the public system.

8. Charles Murray, *In Pursuit of Happiness and Good Government* (New York: Simon and Schuster, 1988), p. 219.

9. *Ibid.*, p. 220.

10. For example, in a graph on p. 221, Murray shows that growth in teachers' salaries has outpaced everyone else—when you consider the "average annual earnings of full-time employees in all industries." There has not been corresponding growth in the quality of education. Quite the reverse.

11. *Ibid.*, p. 224.

12. *Ibid.*, p. 250.

13. The free-market orientation was certainly evident in their approach to education. At the same time, there has recently been a significant liberal movement toward choice. The Brookings Institute, considered a "liberal redoubt," recently issued a report calling for reform of the schools based on "individual control through markets and parental choice." "Use of Free-Enterprise Philosophy Urged for Reform of Public Schools," *Wall Street Journal*, June 5, 1990, A26. *See also* the article on the subject in "Brookings

Report Says Public and Private Schools Should Be Free," *World*, June 16, 1990, pp. 11-12.

14. Nathan Glazer, John Chubb, and Seymour Fliegel, *Making Schools Better* (New York: Manhattan Institute for Policy Research, 1988), pp. 10-11.
15. *Ibid.*, p. 11.
16. *Ibid.*, p. 9.
17. He is now a senior fellow at the Manhattan Institute.
18. *Ibid.*, p. 12.
19. *Ibid.*, p. 17.
20. Myron Lieberman, *The Future of Public Education* (Chicago: University of Chicago Press, 1960), p. 34.
21. Myron Lieberman, *Beyond Public Education* (New York: Praeger Publishers, 1986), p. 2.
22. *See* Kim Lawton, "Bush Clarifies Position on Tuition Tax Credits," *Christianity Today*, May 12, 1989, p. 55 and *Time*, October 9, 1989, p. 69.
23. Susan Tifft, "Some Key Bush Proposals: How They're Doing," *Time*, October 9, 1989, p. 69.
24. Chester Finn, "The Choice Backlash," *National Review*, November 10, 1989, p. 30.
25. Recently, this suffocating paternalism has put forward another argument explaining why, for example, inner-city black kids do so poorly. The argument runs that our education system does not take "cultural diversity" into account. But even granting that diversity, how does it explain the failure? Vietnamese kids have a problem with "cultural diversity" to transcend, and they transcend it. There is, I'm afraid, more than a little racism in the assumption that black kids are incapable of being educated in a culture not their own. And people like Polly Williams are tired of all the nonsense and want to give black children access to schools that will *teach* them.
26. "Teachers vs. Kids," *The Wall Street Journal*, June 6, 1990, p. A16. *See also* Donald Lambro's column in *The Washington Times*, April 5, 1990, F2.
27. Certainly Logos School would have nothing to do with such an arrangement.
28. It does no good to say that if the state's requirements ever require compromise, then the school will leave accreditation behind as too burdensome. The school, while accredited, will almost certainly become dependent on the money that comes as the result of accreditation. Walking away will be far more costly than not walking in.
29. David Harman, *Illiteracy: A National Dilemma* (New York: Cambridge, 1987), p. 61.
30. Rudolf Flesch, *Why Johnny Can't Read* (New York: Harper & Row, 1955), pp. 4-5.
31. *Ibid.*, p. 5.
32. Samuel Blumenfeld, *NEA: Trojan Horse in American Education* (Boise: The Paradigm Company, 1984), pp. 121-122.
33. Rudolf Flesch, *Why Johnny Still Can't Read* (New York: Harper & Row, 1981), p. 1.
34. One question that arises is *why* they persist in such a dumb policy. It is the same question that comes up every time any disastrous policy is stubbornly maintained. The two options are: they do it because they *are* dumb, or they do it because they are diabolical, i.e., they are doing it on purpose.

Blumenfeld appears to opt for the latter explanation. "It was John Dewey who first formulated the notion that high literacy is an obstacle to social-ism." *See* Blumenfeld, *NEA: Trojan Horse*, p. 104.
35. Blumenfeld, *NEA: Trojan Horse*, p. 126.
36. Richard Mitchell, *The Graves of Academe* (Boston-Toronto: Little, Brown, 1981), p. 80.
37. Richard Mitchell, *The Leaning Tower of Babel* (Boston: Little, Brown, 1984), p. 135.
38. *Ibid.*, pp. 222-223.
39. *Ibid.*, p. 221.
40. Richard Powers, *The Dilemma of Education in a Democracy* (Chicago: Regnery Gateway, 1984), p. 11.
41. *Ibid.*, p. 12.
42. *Ibid.*
43. Diane Ravitch and Chester Finn, *What Do Our 17-Year-Olds Know?* (New York: Harper & Row, 1987), pp 102-103.
44. *Ibid.*, p. 54.
45. *Ibid.*, p. 253.
46. *See* Wayne House, ed., *Schooling Choices* (Portland: Multnomah Press, 1988).
47. *Ibid.*, pp. 19-72.
48. Paul Vitz, *Censorship: Evidence of Bias in Our Children's Textbooks* (Ann Arbor: Servant Books, 1986), p. 16.
49. *Ibid.*, p. 11.
50. Vitz also argues that genuine reform will not come until the United States does what every other Western democracy does—support religious schools with public money. He pays particular attention to the "school wars" in Holland in the nineteenth and early twentieth centuries. *Censorship,* pp. 84-88, 95-97.
51. Zena Sutherland and Mary Hill Arbuthnot, *Children and Books* (Glenview, IL: Scott, Foresman, 1977), p. v. The book was also designed for library schools.
52. *Ibid.*, p. 40.
53. *Ibid.*, pp. 45, 50.
54. "Trend Gaining in Public Schools to Add Teaching About Religion," *The New York Times*, March 19, 1989, p. 1.
55. *Ibid.*, p. 1.
56. Paul Parsons, *Inside America's Christian Schools* (Macon, GA: Mercer University Press, 1987), p. 186.
57. *Ibid.*, p. 186.
58. Another recent sop to Christian parents was the June 1990 Supreme Court decision allowing Christian groups equal access to school facilities.
59. Ernest Boyer, "The Third Wave of School Reform," *Christianity Today*, September 22, 1989, p. 16. However, the article unfortunately did not answer the fundamental question about the teaching of morals in public schools. It is, "By what standard do we teach?" The implicit standard assumed in this, an article by a Christian in a Christian magazine, was Utilitarianism.
60. Barrett Mosbacker, ed., *School Based Clinics* (Wheaton, IL: Crossway Books, 1987), p. 173.

NOTES   *193*

61. *Ibid.*, pp. 179-180.
62. *Ibid.*, p. 33.
63. John Whitehead, *Parents' Rights* (Wheaton, IL: Crossway Books, 1985), pp. 105-108.
64. Over half of my property taxes last year went to School District 281. The public school system gets the lion's share.
65. In this regard, our modern humanistic democracy cannot be the means of solving this problem. Frankly, democracy in this sense *is* the problem.
66. In the last year or so, the battle has shifted from the classroom to the football field. The Supreme Court has allowed a ban on pre-game prayer at Douglas County (GA) High School to stand, which has resulted in something of a rebellion all over the South. Frank Trippett, "Throwing God for a Loss," *Time*, September 18, 1989, p. 34.
67. In contrast, private education is no threat to a free society. Not only is it no threat to liberty, it is an expression of liberty. Many proponents of different worldviews enter the field of education (which is a marketplace of ideas) and offer, through private schools, their idea of what education should be. Parents then have the liberty to choose, and no one is being taxed to support a religion they do not believe. Massive public education is consistent with, and will eventually produce, a society in ideological lock-step. A totalitarian society cannot afford liberty in education because it is a root source of all other liberty. A free society, on the other hand, cannot afford to lose its private schools. A loss of freedom in education would be a sign that a loss of general liberty is soon to follow.
68. In 1985 the Supreme Court struck down Alabama's "moment of silence" law because it involved an endorsement and promotion of prayer. Moments of silence are constitutional, but if you don't pray in them, what's the point? Michael Serrill, "Uproar Over Silence," *Time*, June 17, 1985, p. 52.
69. For example, last year the Association of Christian Schools International (ACSI) enjoyed an enrollment increase of 25,000 students over the previous year. (Phone conversation with Paul Kienel, director of ACSI.)
70. R. L. Dabney, *On Secular Education* (Moscow, ID: Ransom Press, 1989), p. 28.
71. Morton Kondrake, "Sorry Summit," *The New Republic*, October 23, 1989, p. 13.

CHAPTER THREE: *The True Ministry of Education*

1. I do not mean to belittle the effective teaching that can occur during devotions. I highly recommend Marian Schoolland, *Leading Little Ones to God* (Grand Rapids: Eerdmans). *Also see* John Abbott, *The Mother at Home* (Sterling, VA: G.A.M. Publications, 1989, 1st. ed., 1833), pp. 69-104.
2. Of course, there is more than just a pragmatic consideration. Some Christians would object to the modern application of such a passage as this on theological grounds, i.e., to require Christian parents to take full responsibility for the education of their children in the sense of this revelation to Moses is to live "under law" and not "under grace." My use of the passage obviously indicates that I believe it (and the rest of Scripture) to be normative (2 Timothy 3:16-17). For the current debate, see Greg Bahnsen,

Theonomy in Christian Ethics (Phillipsburg, NJ: Presbyterian and Reformed Publishing, 1977); Wayne House and Thomas Ice, *Dominion Theology, Blessing or Curse?* (Portland, OR: Multnomah Press, 1988); and Greg Bahnsen and Kenneth Gentry, *House Divided* (Tyler, TX: Institute for Christian Economics, 1989). *See also* John Murray, *Principles of Conduct* (Grand Rapids: Eerdmans, 1957) and Bruce Kay and Gordon Wenham, eds., *Law, Morality and the Bible* (Downers Grove, IL: InterVarsity Press, 1978).

3. C. S. Lewis refers to the modern man's ability to have a dozen incompatible ideas bouncing around in his head. *The Screwtape Letters* (New York: Macmillan, 1961), pp. 7-8. A good education will do much to interfere with such intellectual confusion.

4. Nothing cripples the autonomous defiance of God so much as the realization that each individual was formed a *child*.

5. Parents who provide a Christian education for their children are frequently charged with trying to "shelter" the kids. My response to this is, "Of course, I am sheltering them!" When you think about it, this is a truly *odd* accusation. *O tempora! O mores!* What next? Parents sheltering children!

6. Admittedly some Christians are paranoid about this sort of thing. I once saw a Christian review of *Mary Poppins* that gravely worried about the occultism in it. But on the other side, just because you are paranoid doesn't mean they are *not* out to get you.

7. But parents who are nevertheless interested in pursuing this option should consult Linwood Laughy, *The Interactive Parent* (Kooskia, ID: Mountain Meadow Press, 1988). The book is subtitled *How to Help Your Child Survive and Succeed in the Public Schools.* I would also recommend the newsletter of the American Parents Association, called *Parents in Education.* For more information, write to 1001 Pennsylvania Ave., Suite 850, Washington, DC, 20004.

8. Tony Campolo, *20 Hot Potatoes Christians Are Afraid to Touch* (Waco, TX: Word, 1988), p. 81.

9. Robert Thoburn, *The Children Trap* (Fort Worth, TX: Dominion Press, 1986), p. 143.

10. Victor Porlier, whom I heard at a conference in Spokane, Washington.

11. Josh McDowell, *Where Youth Are Today* (Waco: Word, 1989), film.

CHAPTER FOUR: *The Nature of Knowledge*

1. R. L. Dabney, *On Secular Education* (Moscow, ID: Ransom Press, 1989), p. 17.

2. *Ibid.*, p. 18.

3. The hidden humanist agenda in the public schools is a *transitional* tactic. Once power is consolidated, this agenda becomes overt. Thus the current conflicts in the public schools were not caused by humanists attempting to enter the school system; they came about when the long-present humanism became obvious.

4. Richard Mitchell, *The Leaning Tower of Babel* (Boston: Little, Brown, 1984), p. 95.

5. *Ibid.*, p. 215.

6. Another problem in Mitchell's book is equally glaring. At one point the

author quotes a William Seawell, a professor at the University of Virginia. Professor Seawell stated, "Each child belongs to the state" (p. 272). This upset Mitchell, as well it should. A few pages later Mitchell writes, "To whom then will he turn in the great cause of excellence and the reform of schooling? Plato? Jefferson? To anyone who understands education as the mind's strong defense against manipulation and flattery?" (p. 277).

Those readers who follow Mitchell's advice about thinking should notice something here. On the question of children and the state, Plato and Seawell were kindred spirits. Why does Mr. Mitchell applaud the one and attack the other? Why does he put Plato and Jefferson together? They both had great minds and they are both dead, and that is about the extent of the similarity.

Education is more than being equipped to read Plato, J. S. Mill or Jefferson. It involves teaching students *to think about what they read*. But thinking should include determining whether the author in question was right or wrong—and *that* involves commitment to a standard of truth.

7. Benjamin Wirt Farley, *The Providence of God* (Grand Rapids: Baker, 1988), pp. 43-44.

8. We must be careful with statements like this, however. There are many who state that the Bible is not a textbook of this or that, meaning that the Bible is unreliable at whatever point is under discussion. But while the Bible is not a history "text," all of its history is accurate. While it is not a science "text," it contains nothing in conflict with science.

9. It would be easy to dismiss the charge of chaos in the curriculum as an overstatement. But the intellectual world is in a state of humanistic anarchy, and that anarchy is marching steadily toward kindergarten.

10. Dabney, *On Secular Education*, pp. 16-17.

11. An understanding of theology as the "queen of the sciences" is more than just a pious truism or a throwback to a more naive "age of faith." Before the intellectual world was shattered into its current fragments, theology was considered the queen of the sciences for a *reason*.

12. J. Gresham Machen, *Education, Christianity, and the State* (Jefferson, MD: Trinity Foundation, 1987), p. 81.

13. *Ibid.*, p. 81.

14. C. S. Lewis, *The Abolition of Man* (New York: Macmillan, 1947), p. 13.

15. *See* Paul Vitz, *Censorship: Evidence of Bias in Our Children's Textbooks* (Ann Arbor: Servant Books, 1986), p. 4. When Lewis wrote *The Abolition of Man*, he was prophesying that no good would come of teaching which neglected objective values. When Vitz cited Lewis, the "no good" had already come, seen, and conquered.

16. Lewis, *Abolition of Man*, pp. 16-17.

17. *Ibid.*, p. 14.

18. *Ibid.*, p. 22.

19. Richard Weaver, *Ideas Have Consequences* (Chicago: University of Chicago Press, 1948). Everyone who is serious about applied Christianity should read and reread this book.

20. A cautionary note about "divine purposes" is needed here. As a firm believer in God's exhaustive sovereignty, I believe there is a divine purpose in *all* history. But apart from any revelation from God, we must be extremely cautious about stating what that purpose is. Our lives are mist

(James 4:13-16), and we should not make arrogant pronouncements about God's purposes in history. See also Deuteronomy 29:29.

21. For a contrary view on America's Christian origins, see Noll, Hatch, and Marsden, The Search for Christian America (Wheaton, IL: Crossway Books, 1983). For a dismemberment of their approach, see Gary North, Political Polytheism (Tyler, TX: Institute for Christian Economics, 1989), pp. 222-299. For a discussion of the spirit which sometimes afflicts the writing of some Reconstructionists (like North), see my Law and Love (Moscow, ID: Ransom Press, 1988). North is not in complete disagreement with Noll, Hatch, and Marsden; he argues in Political Polytheism that the Constitution is not what many Christian conservatives believe it to be. See also John Eidsmoe, Christianity and the Constitution (Grand Rapids: Baker, 1987), Gary Amos, Defending the Declaration (Brentwood, TN: Wolgemuth and Hyatt), Forrest McDonald, Novus Ordo Seclorum (Lawrence, KS: University Press of Kansas, 1985), and M. E. Bradford, Remembering Who We Are (Athens, GA: The University of Georgia Press, 1985), pp. 21-44.

22. In conservative Christian circles, America's Christian origin is often thoughtlessly accepted.

23. Gary North, ed., Foundations of Christian Scholarship (Vallecito, CA: Ross House Books, 1979), pp. 159-188. The pages cited are the essay by Vern Poythress on mathematics.

24. A prominent school of Reformed thinking holds that revolutions occur in violation of the Biblical instruction about civil authority in Romans 13:1-7.

25. John Eidsmoe, God and Caesar (Wheaton, IL: Crossway Books, 1984), p. 35.

26. See Arnold Dallimore, George Whitefield (Wheaton, IL: Crossway Books, 1990). While reading this magnificent biography, I came to the conclusion that it would not be too far off to consider George Whitefield the father of our country as well (in a nonpolitical sense). I mentioned this opinion about Whitefield to a student who was about to graduate from the university with a degree in history, and he said, "Who?"

27. My wife teaches American Literature to our tenth grade. For just one more example of the importance of worldviews in education, the impact of evolutionary thinking on writers like Jack London was profound. My wife is able to communicate how important ideas are in the study of literature; to read literature without regard to the worldview of the author destroys the possibility of understanding it.

CHAPTER FIVE: The Student in Adam

1. The image of God has been defaced in man, not effaced. For a good defense of the "mannishness" of man, even fallen man, see Francis Schaeffer, A Christian View of the West, in The Complete Works of Francis A. Schaeffer, vol. 5 (Wheaton, IL: Crossway Books, 1982).

2. J. C. Ryle, Holiness (Greenwood, SC: The Attic Press, 1977), p. 4. On the same page, Ryle observes that "man has many grand and noble faculties left about him, and that in arts and sciences and literature he shows

immense capacity. But the fact still remains that in spiritual things he is utterly 'dead,' and has no natural knowledge, or love, or fear of God."

3. Note that the "dignity of human life" is not the same thing as the "sanctity of human life." A man may be evil and still carry with him the dignity given to him by virtue of the image of God. This has a direct bearing on the abortion controversy, where Christians ought to talk less about the sanctity of human life and more about the sanctity of God's law. Because God's law has sanctity, man has dignity.

4. The Biblical position is sometimes described as "total depravity," which can be misleading. Man is fallen in every aspect of his being, and he is incapable of contributing to his own salvation, but he is not yet at the level of a demon in Hell. Total depravity means total inability, i.e., that man is fallen beyond any hope of contributing to his own salvation. For a good discussion of this, see Boettner, *The Reformed Doctrine of Predestination* (Philadelphia: Presbyterian and Reformed Publishing , 1963), pp. 61-82.

5. Francis Schaeffer, *The Complete Works of Francis A. Schaeffer*, vol. 1 (Wheaton, IL: Crossway Books, 1982), p. 384.

6. C. S. Lewis, *God in the Dock* (Grand Rapids: Eerdmans, 1970), pp. 287-294.

7. G. K. Chesterton, *Orthodoxy* (Garden City, NY: Image Books, 1959), p. 26.

8. If we refuse to mark down poor performance because the child is not *capable* of better, then we have abandoned Biblical dignity in another way. A comment possibly made by C. S. Lewis is to the point: "But once the young people are inside the school, there must be no attempt to establish a factitious egalitarianism between the idlers and dunces on the one hand and the clever and industrious on the other. A modern nation needs a very large class of genuinely educated people, and it is the primary function of schools and universities to supply them. To lower standards or disguise inequalities is fatal." C. S. Lewis, *The Screwtape Letters* (New York: Macmillan, 1982), p. 151. This quote is from a previously unpublished preface to *Screwtape Proposes a Toast*, and I am not at all sure it is Lewis's work. See Kathryn Lindskoog, *The C. S. Lewis Hoax* (Portland, OR: Multnomah Press, 1988). But whether Lewis wrote it or not, the *point* is correct.

9. See Bruce Ray, *Withhold Not Correction* (Phillipsburg, NJ: Presbyterian and Reformed Publishing, 1978). Ray does an outstanding job of presenting Christian parents with a good Biblical description of the task God has given them. While written for parents, Christian teachers would profit from it greatly as well.

10. The *source* of our sin is not our companions, and it is not our environment. The source of our sin is *our* nature, inherited from Adam. This means that Christian schools do not quarantine the students to separate them from sinful companions. The school has a different function altogether.

11. Zena Sutherland and Mary Hill Arbuthnot, *Children and Books* (Glenview, IL: Scott, Foresman, 1977), p. 41. The primer cited was the *New England Primer*, published as early as 1691. It is known to have been in print before that time. The authors of *Children and Books* take a dim view of the primer and of the Puritans in general.

12. One of the difficulties is the curse of superficial solutions. For example, in our losing war against drugs, kids are told to "just say no." Now *there's* a

solution! *Why* should they say no? If we say that they will fry their brains if they take drugs, they respond that they take drugs *to* fry their brains.

13. When an unregenerate child is placed in a Christian school, the increased knowledge he gains of Biblical truth can provoke rebellion against that truth. The other students can see the rebellion, but Christian schools are not instituted to keep our children from seeing sinful behavior. In a good Christian school, such behavior will occur. However, in such a school there is a Biblical consensus about how to deal with it. And of course the students see *that* too.

14. It is ironic that in the area of child-rearing the godly Samuel was bested by the fickle Saul. Samuel had sons who twisted the law of God, while Saul had noble sons—particularly Jonathan.

15. The privileges of children in a Christian home are *covenantal*. See F. W. Grosheide, *The First Epistle to the Corinthians* (Grand Rapids: Eerdmans, 1953), pp. 164-165.

16. The requirement that the children of elders be believers and well-disciplined are surely among the most disobeyed passages of Scripture in the church today. *See* an excellent discussion of how the children of obedient believers will "turn out" in Mary Pride, *The Way Home* (Wheaton, IL: Crossway Books, 1985), pp. 100-105.

17. The approach to work is just *one* example of how a Biblical view of the student affects the operation of the educational process. Tom Garfield comments that a Biblical view of children should be a sobering one for educators. *See* his essay in *No Stone Unturned* (Moscow, ID: Canon Press, 1989), p. 51.

18. This issue of laziness illustrates another difference between a Biblical solution to the education crisis and other suggested solutions. The Christian is not just confronted with problems that need to be solved; he is also confronted with sin that requires repentance.

19. John Milton, *Areopagitica and Of Education* (Northbrook, IL: AHM Publishing, 1951), p. 59.

20. In other words, Christian education is to be the Holy Spirit's instrument, not His substitute. All substitutes for God are spectacular failures, whether they are ecclesiastical, civil, or parental.

21. This discussion is found in the *Gorgias*.

22. Jump several millennia and listen to this: "Consider, for example, the case of education. Is it not almost a self-evident axiom, that the State should require and compel the education, up to a certain standard, of every human being who is born its citizen?" John Stuart Mill, *On Liberty* (New York: Meridian, 1962), p. 238. Mill goes on to argue that the state ought not *provide* a general education, only that it should *require* it. Nevertheless, Mill's trust in what education can do is evident.

23. "What has been will be again, what has been done will be done again; there is nothing new under the sun. Is there anything of which one can say, 'Look! This is something new'? It was here already, long ago; it was here before our time. There is no remembrance of men of old, and even those who are yet to come will not be remembered by those who follow" (Ecclesiastes 1:9-11). Solomon knew all about the follies that currently afflict us.

24. With regard to some of the various ways to understand evil in man, the following comment from Chesterton is apropos. "The ancient masters of reli-

gion were quite easily impressed with that necessity. They began with the fact of sin—a fact as practical as potatoes. Whether or not man could be washed in miraculous waters, there was no doubt at any rate that he wanted washing. But certain religious leaders in London, not mere materialists, have begun in our day not to deny the highly disputable water, but to deny the indisputable dirt. . . . If it be true (as it certainly is) that a man can feel exquisite happiness in skinning a cat, then the religious philosopher can only draw one of two deductions. He must either deny the existence of God, as all atheists do; or he must deny the present union between God and man, as all Christians do. The new theologians seem to think it a highly rationalistic solution to deny the cat." G. K. Chesterton, *Orthodoxy* (Garden City, NY: Image Books, 1959), p. 15.

25. As quoted in Rousas Rushdoony, *Messianic Character of American Education* (Nutley, NJ: Craig Press, 1979), p. 26. For an example of how a humanistic assumption about human nature affects teaching, *see* Sutherland and Arbuthnot, *Children and Books* (Glenview, IL: Scott, Foresman, 1972), pp. 4-17. The first chapter of this book discusses children's needs and how books help to fulfill them. There is a need for physical well-being, a need to love and be loved, a need to belong, etc. There is no need, apparently, to do one's duty to God. The educational process is *child-centered*, not God-centered.

27. The faith is in man *deep down*. With the eyes of faith the humanist looks past all the evil men do, in an attempt to grasp what he truly is. One of the reasons I could not accept the humanist worldview is that it would require more blind faith than I could muster.

28. Stephen Charnock, *The Doctrine of Regeneration* (Grand Rapids: Baker, 1980), p. 8.

29. C. S. Lewis, *Surprised by Joy* (New York: Harcourt, Brace & World, 1955), p. 17.

30. Otto Scott, *James I: The Fool As King* (Vallecito, CA: Ross House Books, 1976), pp. 77, 78. James's mother was Mary Stuart, adversary of John Knox. James Stuart also provides us with a good example of a point made elsewhere in this book: education cannot do the work of regeneration.

31. A more thorough definition of classical education will be provided in an upcoming chapter. For now, it is sufficient to say that a successful classical education provides a rigorous training in basic subjects, done in such a way as to equip the student to learn anything else, along with the desire to continue learning. The student is not given facts *alone*; he or she is given tools.

32. John Milton Gregory, *The Seven Laws of Teaching* (Grand Rapids: Baker, 1979), p. 50.

33. *Ibid.*, p. 23.

34. The same logic lies behind the current efforts to allow for alternative certification for teachers. *See* Susan Tifft, "Some Key Bush Proposals: How They're Doing," *Time*, October 9, 1989, p. 69.

CHAPTER SIX: *The Classical Mind*

1. Russell Kirk, *Enemies of the Permanent Things* (New Rochelle, NY: Arlington House, 1969), pp. 38-39.

2. As a Roman Catholic scholar, Kirk appears to be more open to an intellec-

tual "syncretism" of this sort than evangelical Protestants. Here occurs an interesting phenomenon. When Protestants are classicists, they don't *seem* to be. Roman Catholics tend to be more adept at participating in this "great conversation." A good example from history would be the Puritans, many of whom had a thorough classical education, but who still come across to moderns as Bible-beaters. A friend of mine suggested addressing several problems, including this one, through a change of labels. Those who hold to the theology of the Reformation would be classical Protestants. In response to the Catholic hegemony in classicism, Protestants could be protesting classicists. *I* like it. Classical Protestants and protesting classicists!

3. Mortimer Adler, *Reforming Education* (New York: Collier Books, 1988), p. xxvi. On a side note, Adler takes a strong position on one of the problems presented by classical education. Can classical education be reconciled with universal education? Adler believes it can: "Bloom's book does not manifest the slightest commitment to a program for giving *all* the children the same quality of schooling to enable them to fulfill their common destiny" (p. xxvi). A friend of mine took a somewhat different approach in reconciling the two. He says classical education can be compared to the universal preaching of the gospel where only the elect will respond. The *Trivium* is applied to all; those equipped to really benefit from it will do so, while the others receive a good basic education.

4. One of Charles Williams's novels has a character who refers to encyclopedias as slums for the mind. The point, of course, is that someone who is classically educated does not receive the information second or third hand.

5. George Roche, *A World Without Heroes* (Hillsdale, MI: Hillsdale College Press, 1987), p. 213.

6. John Silber, *Straight Shooting* (New York: Harper and Row, 1989), pp. 48-49.

7. James Schall, *Another Sort of Learning* (San Francisco: Ignatius Press, 1988), pp. 27-28.

8. T. S. Eliot, "Religion and Literature," *Essays Ancient and Modern* (New York: Harcourt, Brace, 1932), p. 109.

9. Allan Bloom, *The Closing of the American Mind* (New York: Simon and Schuster, 1987), pp. 344-347.

10. Russell Kirk, *Decadence and Renewal in the Higher Learning* (South Bend, IN: Gateway Editions, 1978), p. xviii. Kirk is referring to education at the university level, but obviously what is done in the primary and secondary schools has a direct bearing on higher education. As he put it, "Fourth, the enfeeblement of primary and secondary schooling, so that the typical freshman came to enter college wretchedly prepared for the abstractions with which college and university necessarily are concerned." *Ibid.*, p. xiii.

11. And speaking of Whitman, I refer the reader to P. J. O'Rourke, who described him as "a self-obsessed ratchet-jaw with an ear like a tin cookie sheet." P. J. O'Rourke, *Republican Party Reptile* (New York: Atlantic Monthly Press, 1987), p. 6.

12. Even great minds can be led astray by the apparent irrelevance of classical study. John Locke, for example: "When I consider what ado is made about a little Latin and Greek, how many years are spent in it, and what a noise and business it makes to no purpose . . . " John Locke, *On Politics and Education* (Roslyn, NY: Walter J. Black, 1947), p. 331.

13. I am indebted in this section to Francis Kelsey, ed., *Latin and Greek in American Education* (New York: Macmillan, 1911), pp. 17-39 and to Conrad Barrett, "The Importance of Latin and Roman Civilization: Seven Arguments Briefly Stated." The American Classical League, Miami University, Oxford, Ohio 45056.

14. For example, one question was: He knew his *filial* duty. He knew his duty a) as a soldier, b) as an employee, c) as a Christian, or d) as a son. The answer was d. *Filial* comes from the Latin *filius*, which means son.

15. Nancy Mavrogenes, "The Effect of Elementary Latin Instruction on Language Arts Performance," in *Elementary School Journal*, vol. 77, no. 4 (1977): p. 270. The emphasis in the quotation was mine.

16. Kelsey, *Latin and Greek in American Education*, p. 30.

17. Fred Zappfe, "Why Liberal Arts?" *Hadrian's*, August 1989, p. 4.

18. Kelsey, *Latin and Greek in American Education*, p. 24.

19. John Mulder, *The Temple of the Mind* (New York: Pegasus, 1969), p. 23.

20. It is not possible to sustain the charge that this sort of education is incurably elitist, meant only for the sons of the privileged few. ". . . schools under the early Stuarts were remarkably democratic in comparison with those of continental Europe. They were accessible to the sons of landowners, lawyers, doctors, merchants, artisans, and tradesmen. Moreover, they were located in every corner of the realm." This was the work of the Puritans, particularly Cromwell. Mulder continues, "At the time of the Restoration, the country provided one school for every 4,400 of the population. Seven generations later, when a wearied Matthew Arnold inspected the educational system, there was one school for every 23,750 souls." *Ibid.*, p. 14.

CHAPTER SEVEN: *The Trivium and the Christian School*

1. Dorothy Sayers, *The Lost Tools of Learning* (Moscow, ID: Canon Press, 1990), p. 1.

2. *Ibid.*, p. 3.

3. *Ibid.*, p. 4.

4. *Ibid.*, p. 1.

5. *Ibid.*, p. 7.

6. *Ibid.*, p. 9.

7. William Blake, "A Christian Philosophy of Method in Christian Education," *Journal of Christian Reconstruction*, vol. 4, no. 1 (Summer 1977), p. 34.

8. The distinctions between these various levels are not watertight. New facts are always going to be learned (grammar), and it is to be hoped that the student never stops questioning what he reads in the newspaper (dialectic). He should also continue to hone and polish what he learns (rhetoric). Nevertheless, these different elements of the *Trivium* should be very much in evidence at these different grade levels. It is never a question of presence or absence; it is a matter of emphasis. We have structured the school in such a way as to make sure that each level builds on and includes the previous one; we are not interested in isolating them from each other. In addition, as we have learned more about classical education, we have felt free to modify the structure somewhat. Our application of Sayers's insights should not be taken by anyone (including ourselves) as law.

9. John Milton, *Areopagitica and Of Education* (Northbrook, IL: AHM Publishing, 1951), p. 60.
10. *Ibid.*, p. 62.
11. Greg Harris, *The Christian Home School* (Brentwood, TN: Wolgemuth and Hyatt, 1988), p. 39.
12. When we first restructured the PTF, the PTF had one representative on the board. But in the winter of 1990, we modified the structure of the school board. It now has eight members. Three of them are elected by the Logos School Association (parents, patrons, etc.), and the remaining five are permanent. These five permanent board members rotate through four seats on the board. This means that each permanent board member takes a sabbatical every fifth year. Thus the board maintains continuity and the founding vision for the school, and at the same time it is open to new ideas, fresh talent, etc. The PTF still has a large role in the school, but the elected board members now serve a broader constituency, which includes the parents.

CHAPTER EIGHT: *The Obstacles of Modernity*

1. *See* Marie Winn, *The Plug-In Drug* (New York: Bantam Books, 1977), pp. 54-72. Winn points out that even with educational TV, the nature of the learning is quite different from traditional "book learning." Part of the difference involves different levels of *work*. "That it is the availability of television that reduces the amount of reading children do rather than some other factor is easily demonstrated. In the absence of a television set . . . a universal increase in reading, both by parents and by children, is reported. When the less taxing mental activity is unavailable, children turn to reading for entertainment, more willing to put up with the 'work' involved." p. 66.
2. Neil Postman, *Amusing Ourselves to Death* (New York: Penguin Books USA, 1985), p. 147.
3. *Ibid.*
4. *Ibid.*, p. 148.
5. *Ibid.*
6. *Ibid.* The emphasis is mine.
7. For a less critical discussion of educational TV, see Liebert, Sprafkin, and Davidson, *The Early Window* (New York: Pergamon Press, 1982), pp. 180-211. *See also* Edward Palmer, ed., *Children and the Faces of Television* (New York: Academic Press, 1980), pp. 1-108.
8. Nancy Wilson, "The Great Debates: Is MTV Harmful to Kids, Teenagers?" *The Daily Idahonian*, weekend edition, November 8/9, 1986. p. 4.
9. The didactic force of TV is also seen in the impact violent programs have on children. *See* Barlow and Hill, eds., *Video Violence and Children* (New York: St. Martin's Press, 1985), p. 13.
10. Allan Bloom, *The Closing of the American Mind* (New York: Simon and Schuster, 1987), p. 79.
11. *Ibid.*, p. 81.

CHAPTER NINE: *The Problem of "Pious" Ignorance*

1. T. S. Eliot argues that the classics should be studied as a means of *preserving* Christian civilization. His essay is called "Modern Education and the

Classics," in *Essays Ancient and Modern* (New York: Harcourt, Brace, 1932), pp. 169-185.

2. There is a famous saying to this effect in Tertullian, *On Prescription Against Heretics*, *The Ante-Nicene Fathers*, vol. 3 (Grand Rapids: Eerdmans, 1989), p. 246. "What indeed has Athens to do with Jerusalem? What concord is there between the Academy and the Church? What between heretics and Christians? Our instruction comes from 'the porch of Solomon,' who had himself taught that 'the Lord should be sought in simplicity of heart.' Away with all attempts to produce a mottled Christianity of Stoic, Platonic, and dialectic composition!" It bears mentioning that Tertullian's warm piety and "simplicity of heart" was insufficient protection against the heresy of Montanism, which he embraced later in life.

3. C. S. Lewis, "Christianity and Culture," *Christian Reflections* (Grand Rapids: Eerdmans, 1967), p. 15.

4. *Ibid.*, p. 17.

5. For an argument that Paul did possess a considerable degree of eloquence, see Augustine, *On Christian Doctrine*, bk. 4, Great Books Series, vol. 18 (Chicago: William Benton, 1952), pp. 678-682. It is interesting to note that in this book Augustine has to defend the *lawfulness* of rhetoric. This controversy has been with us for a while.

6. The taking captive of every thought could be considered part of the cultural mandate given to Adam and Eve in Genesis 1:28. Although sin affects how the mandate is to be fulfilled, God never revoked the mandate because of sin. In fact, the mandate appears to be given again after the flood (Genesis 9:1). There is no way to fulfill this cultural mandate apart from education.

7. Samuel T. Logan, *The Preacher and Preaching* (Phillipsburg, NJ: Presbyterian and Reformed Publishing, 1986), p. 321. An outstanding treatment of classicism and Christianity (at least for preachers) can be seen in R. L. Dabney, *R. L. Dabney on Preaching: Lectures on Sacred Rhetoric* (Edinburgh: Banner of Truth Trust, 1979). Even though I am writing a book on education, my citation of two sources dealing with preaching is not beside the point. If a classical education can be used to advance the evangelical proclamation, there should be no problem for Christians elsewhere.

8. The intelligence to be found there can also be extremely foolish. Some of the most foolish ideas will find more adherents among the educated than anywhere else. Evolutionary atheism and Marxism are just two examples. A good commentary on the educated class can be seen in C. S. Lewis, *That Hideous Strength* (New York: Macmillan, 1943), pp. 99-100. "Why you fool, it's the educated reader who *can* be gulled. All our difficulty comes with the others. When did you meet a workman who believes the papers? He takes it for granted that they're all propaganda and skips the leading articles. He buys his paper for the football results and the little paragraphs about girls falling out of windows and corpses found in Mayfair flats. He is our problem. We have to recondition him. But the educated public, the people who read the highbrow weeklies, don't need reconditioning. They're all right already. They'll believe anything."

9. I am indebted here to Leland Ryken, *Worldly Saints* (Grand Rapids: Zondervan, 1986), pp. 156-171.

10. This is a profound truth, but like all truth it can be badly handled. To say that all truth is God's truth is *not* to say there is such a thing as "neutral

truth," or "autonomous truth." There have been many who, when proclaiming that "all truth is God's truth," have thrown out God's revealed truth in Scripture on the basis of some "truth" they claim to have found somewhere else. General revelation must submit to special revelation.

11. Ryken, *Worldly Saints*, p. 167.
12. Cotton, as quoted in *ibid.*, p. 168.
13. Timothy Dowley, ed., *Eerdmans Handbook to the History of Christianity* (Grand Rapids: Eerdmans, 1977), p. 43. The Royal Society was founded in 1661.
14. Ryken, *Worldly Saints*, p. 158.
15. *Ibid.*
16. For an interesting study on the extent of Solomon's wisdom, see Thomas Johnston, *Did the Phoenicians Discover America?* (Houston: St. Thomas Press, 1965).

CHAPTER TEN: *The Home School Alternative*

1. For example, the average circulation of *The Teaching Home* last year was around 30,000. This figure is only a fraction of those who are home schooling. Those interested in subscribing should write to *The Teaching Home*, P.O. Box 20219, Portland OR 97220-0219.
2. A conversation with Mike and Mary Lou Nadreau.
3. Wayne House, ed., *Schooling Choices* (Portland, OR: Multnomah, 1988), p. 253.
4. It is important to note the emphasis I place on the *average* home. Of course, there will always be exceptional parents, fully equipped to educate their exceptional children. But we are not discussing the education of John Stuart Mill; rather, we are concerned with the education as it should be practiced in the average Christian home.
5. Gregg Harris, *The Christian Home School* (Brentwood, TN: Wolgemuth and Hyatt, 1988), p. 44.
6. *Ibid.*
7. *Ibid.*
8. *Ibid.*
9. She is currently a part-time English teacher in our secondary program. Two of her students have been our oldest daughter and our son. I have taught Latin and Bible to our daughter as well, and Latin and Bible to our son. It is sort of a private school/home school co-op.
10. Raymond and Dorothy Moore, *Home-spun Schools* (Waco, TX: Word Books, 1982), pp. 14-15.
11. Even when parents are guilty of educational malpractice such as this, it is still important to maintain the principle that education is a parental responsibility and that the state should not usurp it. Many parents feed their kids Twinkies all the time too, but we don't need a State Bureau of Nutrition Requirements. The cure must not be worse than the disease.
12. Borg Hendrickson, *Home School: Taking the First Step* (Kooskia, ID: Mountain Meadow Press, 1989), p. 23.
13. I am defining home school as a situation where the teaching is done by the parents. If the teaching is in any way farmed out, then the result will be some sort of school. It may not be a traditional school, but it is a school. I

am defining a school as any educational situation in which parents utilize a division of labor in teaching to any significant degree.

14. The more division of labor there is, the more it is necessary for parents to be diligent in this oversight. But the work necessary for responsible oversight of a child's *Christian* teachers is far less than the work necessary to do that teaching oneself.

15. Mary Pride, *The Big Book of Home Learning* (Wheaton, IL: Crossway Books, 1986; now Volumes 1-4, 1990, 1991). The book is a treasure trove of information about "everything educational for you and your children." It was here that we first found out about some of the Latin texts that Logos uses for the elementary grades. The texts are for junior high level, but we have been able to use them for fifth and sixth grade.

16. We would also home school if we were unable to afford the tuition of a Christian school. I believe those who home school because of financial constraints demonstrate true commitment to their children. They resist the temptations of a "free" education at the public school, and with limited resources, assume the responsibilities God gave them.

17. There is one other argument for Christian schools that can be made as well. Inefficiency results from a poor use of division of labor. The resultant inefficiency is using up a lot of Christian talent desperately needed elsewhere. If a good teacher, under parental oversight, can do as good a job for ten children as ten mothers would, then couldn't that free up the mothers to volunteer in crisis pregnancy centers, etc.?

18. Alberta Griffiths, "Ethnographic Perspectives of Selected Home School Families in Pennsylvania" (Ph.D. diss., Lehigh University, 1988), pp. 57-60.

CHAPTER ELEVEN: *The Limits of the State: A Summary*

1. Paul Copperman, as quoted in *A Nation at Risk*, National Commission on Excellence in Education, (Washington, DC: U. S. Government Printing Office, 1983), p. 11.

2. NEA Legislative Information (news release), Testimony of the National Education Association Before the Labor and Human Resources Committee of the U.S. Senate, Presented by Mary Hatwood Futrell, NEA President, February 18, 1987.

3. That board has now been formed and is producing material written in educationese. *See* National Board for Professional Teaching Standards, *Toward High and Rigorous Standards for the Teaching Profession* (Detroit: NBPTS, 1989). I noted the second of three reform proposals on p. 60. "Increasing the supply of high quality entrants into the profession, with special emphasis on minorities." *Nothing* is changing in the establishment.

4. For just a small sampling, see George Gilder, *Wealth and Poverty* (New York: Basic Books, 1981), Frederic Bastiat, *The Law* (Irvington-On-Hudson, NY: The Foundation for Economic Education, 1950), Friedrich Hayek, *The Road to Serfdom* (Chicago: University of Chicago Press, 1944), and Ronald Nash, *Poverty and Wealth* (Wheaton, IL: Crossway Books, 1986). I would also recommend Adam Smith, Von Mises, and Milton Friedman.

5. The problem with "look/say" was touched on in the second chapter. This method treats English words, which can be sounded out, as though they were Chinese characters, which cannot be. This complex squiggle represents a chair, for some reason, and that complex squiggle represents a church. In the study of phonics, children learn the sounds of the various letters and combinations of letters. They are then taught to decode new words from left to right. With "look/say," brighter students can teach themselves phonics ("Oh, *ch* has the same sound in both these words!"). But many students are totally at sea and are later diagnosed as "learning impaired." The real problem is that the public schools are teaching impaired.

6. The adjective *strict* is necessary because not everyone who claims to be teaching phonics is actually doing so. Advocates of true phonics instruction will also sometimes identify the approach as one of teaching "intensive phonics."

7. *See* Thomas Smith, *Educating for Disaster* (Evanston, NY: UCA Books, 1986). The subtitle is *The Nuclear Spectre in America's Classrooms.* Smith argues that children in the public schools are hostages to a left-wing political agenda.

8. Mel and Norma Gabler, *What Are They Teaching Our Children?* (Wheaton, IL: Victor Books, 1985).

9. Charles Murray, *In Pursuit of Happiness and Good Government* (New York: Simon and Schuster, 1988), p. 203. On the next page, Murray goes on to cite the fact that "graduates who took the Graduate Record Examination (GRE) intending to major in education during graduate school—in other words, those who will be running the school systems of the future—the GRE-Verbal score put them in the bottom third of new graduate students."

10. That there are such good teachers is clear. Consider this testimony of the problem, along with the evidence that it is not a universal problem. "Consider that, nationally, the combined 1988 SAT score among students intending to study education is 855, a full 49 points below the national mean of 904 for all college-bound students. . . . Boston University's School of Education has successfully resisted this change. We raised our combined SAT average of those preparing for careers in teaching to 1090 by 1988, which is 235 points above the 1988 national mean for students intending to study education." John Silber, *Straight Shooting* (New York: Harper and Row, 1989), p. 19.

11. Some may object that some of the reforms (vouchers, tuition tax credits, etc.) *do* address the problem of lack of competition for the schools. But for the most part, such reforms do not go far enough to produce a true free market in education.

CHAPTER TWELVE: *The Need for Classical and Christian Education: A Summary*

1. C. S. Lewis, *The Abolition of Man* (Toronto: Macmillan, 1947), p. 35.

APPENDIX C

1. For two revealing books on the background and history of public education in America, see Rousas Rushdoony, *The Messianic Character of American*

Education (Nutley, NJ: Craig Press, 1979) and Samuel Blumenfeld, *Is Public Education Necessary?* (Boise: The Paradigm Company, 1985).

2. Plato, *The Republic* (Chicago: Encyclopedia Britannica, 1952), p. 295.

3. For an account of utopianism in the twentieth century, see Rael Jean and Erich Isaac, *The Coercive Utopians* (Chicago: Regnery Gateway, 1983).

4. For the classic Christian work on the City of Man and the City of God, see Augustine, *The City of God* (New York: The Modern Library, 1950). There are many editions available. Augustine was treating the City of Man in the twilight of paganism; we are dealing with a resurgent neo-paganism. The principle is the same.

5. Marx and Engels, *The Communist Manifesto*, Great Book Series, vol. 50 (Chicago: University of Chicago, 1952), p. 427

6. *Ibid.*, p. 429.

7. In the same way, few modern statist educators in America are Marxist. Still, it is interesting to note how often they interact with Marxist theory in their books. For example, see Feinberg and Soltis, *School and Society* (New York: Teachers College Press, 1985), pp. 43-56. For a Marxist analysis of the crisis in education, see Madan Sarap, *Education, State and Crisis* (London: Routledge and Kegan Paul, 1982).

8. The recent events in eastern Europe indicate that communism is dead where it has been tried. But it is not dying in the minds of intellectuals in the West. Nor is statism in American education discredited. The performance of the schools is discredited, but people do not yet blame the system the way the people in communist countries blame the system.

9. R. L. Dabney, *On Secular Education* (Moscow: Ransom Press, 1989), pp. 29-30.

10 Samuel Blumenfeld, *NEA: Trojan Horse in American Education* (Boise: The Paradigm Company, 1984), pp. 1-8.

11. Thomas McCrie, *The Story of the Scottish Church* (Glasgow: Free Presbyterian Publications, 1988).

12. Samuel Blumenfeld, *Is Public Education Necessary?* (Boise: The Paradigm Company, 1985), pp. 37-42.

13. Horace Mann, as quoted in Rushdoony, *Messianic Character of American Education*, p. 29.

14. J. Gresham Machen, *Education, Christianity and the State* (Jefferson, MD: The Trinity Foundation, 1987), pp. 92, 104-5.

15. *Ibid.*

16. Many Christians and assorted traditionalists view the NEA and the educational establishment as perverting the original purpose of public education in America This is not true; they are the fulfillment of it. It has taken a while for the radical nature of the premises to become manifest.

The reason it has taken a long time for the agenda of the radicals to come to fruition is because of the strong influence of Christianity in the United States. But there should be no mistake. Radicalism has been part of the agenda from day one. A good example is the Department of Education. President Jimmy Carter gave the NEA their cabinet level position during his tenure of office. But this federal department has been a goal of the NEA since that organization was formed in 1857.

SELECT BIBLIOGRAPHY

Augustine. *On Christian Doctrine*. Great Books of the Western World Series, vol. 18. Chicago: William Benton, 1952, pp. 621-698.

Bloom, Allan. *The Closing of the American Mind*. New York: Simon and Schuster, 1987.

Blumenfeld, Samuel. *Is Public Education Necessary?* Boise, ID: The Paradigm Company, 1981.

Dabney, R. L. *On Secular Education*. Moscow, ID: Ransom Press, 1989.

Flesch, Rudolf. *Why Johnny Can't Read*. New York: Harper & Row, 1955.

Gregory, John. *The Seven Laws of Teaching*. Grand Rapids: Baker, 1979.

Lewis, C. S. *The Abolition of Man*. New York: Macmillan, 1947.

Machen, J. Gresham. *Education, Christianity, and the State*. Jefferson, MD: Trinity Foundation, 1987.

Milton, John. *Areopagitica and Of Education*. Northbrook, IL: AHM Publishing, 1951.

Powers, Richard. *The Dilemma of Education in a Democracy*. Chicago: Regnery Gateway, 1984.

Rushdoony, Rousas. *The Messianic Character of American Education*. Nutley, NJ: Craig Press, 1979.

Sayers, Dorothy. *The Lost Tools of Learning*. Moscow, ID: Canon Press, 1990.

Weaver, Richard. *Ideas Have Consequences*. Chicago: University of Chicago Press, 1948.

SCRIPTURE INDEX

GENERAL INDEX